Tuck Your Skirt in Your Panties and Run

Lucy Adams 1/24/11

Tuck Your Skirt in Your Panties and Run!

Lucy Adams

Palm Tree Press
Atlanta

To Sarah Kelly
I never meant any harm

Table of Contents

Introduction
Dear Ms. Kelly
xi

Chapter One
The Girl in Cornflower Blue
1

Chapter Two
Weaving a Tangled Web
31

Chapter Three
The Dog Years of Marriage
61

Chapter Four
Chain of Fools
83

Chapter Five
Almost Famous
115

Chapter Six
Variations on a Variorium
143

Postlogue
Dainty Leave-Taking
165

About the Author
169

Acknowledgements
170

Introduction

Dear Ms. Kelly

"Why don't they do a reality TV show about a married, hetero, middle class couple with kids, a dog, and a few goldfish swimming in a tank. The dad works hard. The mom works hard. They get along with their extended family. Their kids are pretty good, all things considered," my beloved complained.

"Because," I enlightened him, "it's too boring. People thrive off of chaos and controversy. They want to watch mayhem and destruction. They want to see other people running with their skirts tucked in their panties so they can feel better about their own lackluster lives."

When the going gets tough, or downright embarrassing, that's when I tuck my skirt in my panties and run. I hightail it out of there before I have to face the music. Sometimes, however, I'm not so lucky and I face the disaster du jour before I get my skirt all the way into my panties and get a move on. On, thankfully, rare occasions, someone tucks my skirt in my panties for me, slaps me on the butt, and says, "Now git on outa here."

As an example of the latter, consider this real letter from a real reader of my weekly newspaper column:

I recently read your article, That's Life, in the True Citizen and was just appalled. I have sent a letter to the editor of the newspaper which I have attached to this e-mail. Just in case it is not printed, I still want you to know how disgusting your article is. Thank you for your time.

Admittedly, I was flattered that she had the nerve to scathingly insult me and then thank me for my time. I now know she thanked me because she wanted me to open the attachment and give her another shot at affronting me. It worked:

Editor:

Recently I read an article in the June 12 edition of the True Citizen *which simply embarrassed me. The article by Lucy Adams entitled That's Life told of an overweight woman Ms. Adams encountered while at the beach. I don't believe I have ever been so infuriated by a short, and ultimately meaningless, editorial.*

First of all, Ms. Adams, have you recently run out of insecurities of your own to write about; have you now had to resort to blatantly and publicly ridiculing other people in your weekly article? I don't know of anyone who would make such derogatory statements, in a newspaper nonetheless, about the weight of a random stranger. Obviously you have more audacity than most people, or is it simply a lack of morality? Perhaps that lady has a disease which caused her to gain weight, or maybe she is just comfortable with who she is. I would like nothing more than to joke about some of the physical characteristics I immediately took notice of when seeing your picture by that article, if for no other reason than for the justice of the woman you wrote about; however, like you, my mother taught me better than that. You may want to buy a fan for that "short track" you're on, Ms. Adams.

Finally, I am astonished and ashamed that the True Citizen *would print an article of such content. I've often wondered if anyone proof-reads anything printed in the paper, and now I suppose I don't have to wonder anymore because I honestly cannot believe that someone read That's Life and printed it anyway. What happened to writing about meaningful subjects? What a concept! I am fairly positive that the is-sues of war, starvation, disease, and natural disasters are popular; maybe someone could look into that.*

Needless to say, I was stunned. Although I took the audacity attribu-tion as a compliment, because in reality I am a non-confrontational, don't-rock-the-boat, fly-under-the-radar wimp, the rest of it left me absolutely speechless. Instead of wanting to read about my run-in with an unlikely, but enlightening, role model, this lady wanted to read about death, dis-ease, and destruction.

Besides that, she had taken the hem of my skirt and shoved it so hard into the elastic of my bloomers, she gave me wedgy. To top it off, she planted her foot firmly on my backside and shoved me into the next coun-ty. Of course, not to prove her wrong about her audacity comment, but in true character, I responded thusly:

Dear Ms. Kelly,

I regret that my column, That's Life, struck a negative chord with you. As always, I appreciate that subscribers to the **True Citizen,** *such as yourself, read my column, and never do I write one word with the goal of intentionally offending readers. Unfortunately, due to the nature of my business, I run the risk of submitting to newspapers opinions that not everyone may find agreeable.*

Please also allow me the opportunity to clarify why I wrote the col-umn: I recognized that I was laughing at something I shouldn't. Then I noticed that the ladies were laughing at themselves. The lesson I learned from the situation is that when I am wallowing in the troubles of life, instead of taking myself too seriously, I need to laugh and allow others to laugh at my expense. The chance to bring lightheartedness to people is a gift and a blessing to be recognized and cherished.

Thank you for sharing your concern with me, and please continue to read.

Sincerely,
Lucy Adams

I may as well have written back, *Blah, blah, blah,* because I feel certain that she didn't keep reading and that she still didn't understand what she had read in the first place. And frankly, I was ticked at myself for not developing a better come-back than that. At long last, I finally have:

Dear Ms. Kelly,

It has come to my attention that some readers misinterpret, misuse, and/ or attempt to repurpose this column. Therefore, my attorney of record advised me to write a blanket disclaimer and warning statement. It follows:

Please read all information regarding the inherent dangers of this product as well as how to use this product safely and effectively.

Caution! Contents hot!

You could be a winner! Details inside.

Actual column is not this size. Objects and subjects may appear larger than life. Purchase does not include children or pets named herein. Woman pictured not included with product. May contain nuts or nut by-products. May have been manufactured by a nut, near a nut, or with a nut.

Not intended for personal hygiene use. Not to be used in bathrooms. Keep well away from mucous membranes. For external use only. Do not use in shower.

Do not use for drying pets. Don't feed to fish. Not for use by animals, namely puppies and birds.

Do not turn upside down.

Do not eat. Do not swallow. If ingestion occurs, contact physician immediately. Serving suggestion is only a suggestion and not mandatory.

Do not attempt to drive vehicle with this device in place. Do not engage while vehicle is in motion. Not intended for highway use. Do not use while operating machinery.

Any unauthorized use of this product, either intentional or unintentional, may result in injury. If torn, may contain sharp edges. Not responsible for paper cuts or other damages incurred from improper use, distribution, handling, clipping, etc. Misuse may result in paralysis, blindness, headaches, nausea, slow healing wounds, backaches, tooth decay, or jail time.

Smoking while using this product may result in fire. Do not use near flame or spark. Not intended to be used to ignite fire. Do not place lit candles on this surface.

May cause drowsiness. May cause fatigue. Do not use while sleeping or unconscious.

Do not use if you cannot see clearly. Do not use as earplugs.

Do not dangle or throw at co-workers.

Do not insert this product into any electronic equipment.

Some, all, or a smidgen of this product may be recycled.

This product cannot protect any part of the body it doesn't cover. This product cannot protect any part of the body it does cover. This is not a safety protective device. Not to be used as a personal flotation device.

Not intended for use as a dental drill or educational tool.

May contain small parts. Not intended for children under 3. Keep out of reach of children and teenagers. Remove infant before folding for storage.

Not for weight control. Does not enable one to fly.

Not dishwasher safe.

When placed on ice, this may be cold. Defrost.

One size fits all. This is not underwear. Do not attempt to put in pants.

This product may cause irritation. Results are typical.

Professional writer. Do not attempt at home.

Do not use on the roof.

This product has been known to cause uncontrollable laughter in laboratory mice. No animals were harmed in the making of this product.

For best results, remove wrapper, unfold, and read.

This material should be approached with an open mind, studied carefully, and critically considered. It may offend some of the people some of the time. Comes with no guarantee. Readers are encouraged to fully consider evidence for and evidence against these ideas.

Offending sections should be removed with a razor blade. Unauthorized use of a razor blade to alter this product in any way renders null and void any warranty, actual or implied.

That will tuck Ms. Kelly's skirt for sure . . . maybe . . . if there is any chance at all that she will read this book. Alas, it is so me to think of the perfect rejoinder when the moment has passed, long, long ago.

For the rest of y'all, and Ms. Kelly, too, if she decides to give me another chance and participate, I promise you will read nothing about war, starvation, disease, or natural disasters, except those disasters which naturally happened to me, or I naturally observed, or I naturally heard about from a friend of a friend. And it will honor me greatly if you laugh at my insecurities, my frailties, and my flaws.

I give you, *Tuck Your Skirt in Your Panties and Run*, at my expense; real stories about real people doing real things and some of the things they do are real stupid. If you don't like the stories, if they offend you, well then, I'm sorry, but that's life.

Lucy Adams
Thomson, GA
June 15, 2009

Chapter One
The Girl in Cornflower Blue

It was a wonderful wedding reception regardless of how conspicuous I felt at my age, wearing a bridesmaid dress and all. At least it was blue and I had a tan and for awhile I fooled myself into thinking almost 40 isn't so old. But half a glass of wine away from sneaking off to smoke with the help, I caught my image in the mirror over the bar. It said, "You can't take a drag off a single cigarette no matter how young and rebellious it might make you feel. You have your life insurance policy to consider. Suppose you keel over dead and when they perform the autopsy they discover traces of nicotine in your blood. You're listed as a non-smoker. The insurance company will refuse to pay the claim. You'll leave your family destitute."

Damn, almost forty might not be so old, but it's way past the point of wild abandon.

The Girl in Cornflower Blue

It's the kind of thing a girl over a certain age does only for the women in her life whom she loves the very best. Otherwise, she makes an excuse like, "You know I would do anything for you, but Weight Watchers quarantined me, indefinitely."

For a true friend, however, she layers on the Spanx, wears a serious Wonderbra, slips on the three-inch Thom McCann's, and buys a brace for each ankle. There are just some friends she would be in their wedding, even if she had to drag her oxygen tank behind her down the aisle.

That's what Stephanie and I share in common. We've both step-stopped, step-stopped, step-stopped to the altar, ahead of a beaming bride, well after the age of when groomsmen gaze across the aisle hoping to hook-up at the reception. Every thirty-nine year-old in a clingy, strapless, silk bridesmaid gown asks herself the same neurotic question: *Does this dress transform me into daringly young and attractive or is everyone thinking, Poor dear. Looks like she got a bad plastic surgery job?*

To be that old, standing before the wedding guests, flanking a stunning vision in white, can cause a lady to feel like her girdle slipped, webbing her thighs together and letting a ring of flesh conspicuously bubble out and roll beneath the filmy fabric of her gown.

So, though her friends may laugh, Stephanie reacted quite normally when the driver of a white van, which pulled beside the car transporting the bride's attendants from the wedding to the reception, rested his eyes on her for an unusual length of time. She met his stare and looked away, flirtatiously smoothing and flipping her hair. "This guy is checking me out, y'all," she delightedly announced to the other girls.

Oh my gosh, this guy is really checking me out. I look good, she praised herself and glanced down at her chest, giving it a discreet boost. Surreptitiously, she peeked again in the man's direction.

That's when she saw the wording on the van: PUMP AND DUMP PLUMBERS, 706-BIG-PIPE. *Well, it figures,* she disappointedly mused, forgetting her posture. Her fantasy included George Clooney, not Edwayne, as the red oval on his shirt identified him. Almost immediately, she conjured a vision of Edwayne bent over under her vanity sink, his pants revealing more flesh than she could tolerate. *Turn green, light,* she wished. *Pleeease turn green.*

The fellow waved to get her attention. *Don't look,* she coached herself. *It'll encourage him. Oh heck, he's rolling down his window. Light, pleeeeeease turn green.*

"Ma'am!"

She didn't acknowledge his salutation.

"Ma'am!" he called, a little louder.

She willed herself to stare straight ahead.

"Hey lady!" he gestured and pointed. "Your dress is caught!"

She at last turned toward him, confused.

"Your dress!" he repeated. "You closed your door on it!"

The light turned green, and the Good Samaritan drove away, as an embarrassed Stephanie reeled in her crinkled crinoline, yelling after him, "But I'm still pretty, right?"

I've been there; the girl in cornflower blue, my Spanx squeezing me so tightly, oxygen deprivation pushed me within one glass of wine away from chatting up the help, just to manipulate them into telling me how good I made that dress look. But in retrospect, Stephanie and I didn't really need the affirmation of plumbers or bar-keeps, because women like us, willing to bind up our egos in all array of undergarments for our dearest friends, we are still pretty. Right?

And guys like Edwayne? They aren't so bad either.

It's Better to Burn Out than Fade Away

"**W**hy are you so edgy, lately," he asked.

"Our daughter, the child who's supposed to be on the pink team with me," I responded, "asked if I'm old. She observed 'crunks' on my face."

"Crunks," he quizzed.

"Yes, lines, creases, wrinkles," I translated. "Do you know my birthday is coming up in November? What have I accomplished, other than mastering the daily grind?" I looked at my hands resting in my lap. "I think I'm having a midlife crisis."

"You're not old enough," he tried to mollify me.

I argued, "None of us knows where we are on our personal timelines. I could have passed the halfway mark years ago, without feeling the bump."

A dark silence fell. This particular field of thought unnerved my optimistic-against-all-odds spouse.

"I don't just want to leave my mark on the world," I eventually continued. "That's for sissies. I want to kick a dent so deep that the sands of time can't ever fill it."

What can a man say after his wife confesses such deep discontent with the status quo? The subject dropped off an invisible cliff.

No doubt, however, it preyed upon my husband, gnawing at his sensibilities. For my birthday, he decided to thump me out of my funk, and surprised me with tickets to a Def Leppard show. Like a hypnotist, he wanted to take me back, before children, before marriage, before college, before I acknowledged my mortality.

After balking, I gave in and purchased my gig gear - one blue lighter - shoved it deep in my pocket, threw my fists in the air, thumbs, index fingers, and pinkies extended, and exclaimed, "Let's rock!"

In the dark coliseum, Def Leppard's drums and bass guitar vibrated my chest cavity, forever altering my cardiac rhythm. The crowd of thirty and forty-somethings roared in response to the lyrics, *Is anybody out there?!!!* I held a flame over my head, swaying; a concert ritual that I honestly don't understand, and that most fans have given up, tendering illuminated cell phones instead.

"No matter," I impatiently said to the temporarily suppressed practical matron creeping around my psyche, who annoyingly kept rapping on my skull and asking why old guitar players wear their hair so big and have loops of chain dangling from their pants, and why every song includes the word "rock" in some form, and complaining about the dangers of fireballs shooting from the stage.

Seeing me caught in the moment, my spouse leaned in and yelled, "We're so cool! We're rebels! It's a Thursday night! We have to work tomorrow!"

"We're not cool if we have to say we're cool," I shouted back, fumbling for the lighter, wishing to restore my concert persona.

He attempted to erase his faux pas. "Let's get tattoos after this!"

"Pour some sugar on me . . .," I sang louder.

Walking through the corridor after the encore, still mouthing, "It's better to burn out, yeah, than fade away . . .," we passed the t-shirt booth. Eyes always peeled, my spouse spotted a pair of black, leather, thong-style, band-panties, hanging on the display. With a grin on his face and his wallet out, he bumped me with his elbow and pointed.

"Considering the average age of the crowd," I dryly retorted, "they ought to sell big, white granny-panties."

No, the event didn't ease my need for cracking the earth wide open, but Def Leppard did rock our aging faces off, with a lot less expense and pain than plastic surgery. And I thank my ever faithful mate for putting the funky in my birthday funk.

Radio Head

Radio will love your face, he plied me. And I swallowed that compliment like a shot of white lightnin' fresh from the distillery. Even so, with my right arm twisted ruthlessly behind my back, I halfheartedly agreed to give it a go.

As a result, I recently made my radio debut voicing a ninety second spot for a close associate, a wedding consultant extraordinaire. He wanted to hire a local celebrity to convey to brides the vast joy they will feel when he organizes and implements their weddings. All he could afford, however, was me.

After meticulously recording twenty-nine re-takes, discovering that some people don't appreciate dramatic interpretation, and failing at divaishly commanding my pal to paint my toenails, put my name on the back of my chair and bring me a co-cola, I finally floated my delicate Southern accent over America's airwaves; all the while, concealing the deep fear in my gut that people might recognize my voice.

In return for my services, I find myself in the unusual circumstance of opening an umbrella against the hailstorm brewed by my little blurb, which goes something like this:

It's a new year and time to start planning your upcoming nuptials. Your special day is a once in a lifetime event. [Blah, blah, blah] We provide top of the line service to set the perfect mood and take the headache out of planning, so you can enjoy your wedding. [Blah, blah, blah, blah, blah] Our staff will recommend reception sites, caterers, florists, [blah, blah, and blah, blah]. Make us the first stop on your journey to a lifetime of bliss.

I'll never understand how that last line, *Make us the first stop on your way to a lifetime of bliss*, an innocent suggestion, created such contention. Nevertheless, now, after the initial airing of my fantasy vault to fame (or, more accurately, infamy), the public buzzes with debates over whether I engaged in false and misleading statements.

Anonymous crank calls come in like clockwork, with women at the end of the line telling me, "I enjoy hearing your lovely voice on the radio, but lifetime of bliss? Give me a break." Other callers amen this sentiment, saying, "You foul mouthed tart!"

One caller claims she doesn't understand what I mean by "once in a lifetime" or "bliss," or how those things have anything to do with weddings.

Discontent struck the men, as well, in due course. Sick of hearing their mates pooh-pooh me, and, thus, them, every time my ad rotates on the radio line-up, several husbands have slyly discovered that their wives failed to hire my friend. Consequently, these men now point fingers accusingly at me. They say happiness was never knowing that bliss could have been bought.

(There's something to be said for both customer service and maiming the messenger.)

With the weight of the wedded world upon my weedy shoulders, I asked my chum how much longer he plans to use that particular commercial. He proclaims the year is still young. I suspect, secretly, he feels a bit like the Wizard of Oz, handing out hearts to those who dare request one.

Therefore, the great and wonderful Oz abandoned me, singing *If I only had a brain*, to defend myself from the mama and paparazzi. So like any starlet stumbling in a bed of bad PR, I declare to one and all, "Darlings, I don't write the lines, I just make them memorable." (Which is only half true, if true at all, because my friend couldn't afford a writer either, so...)

But there I go, letting fifteen seconds feel like forever, and getting a big radio head.

The Constellation Prize

My students galloped from P.E. gaily chirping about "constellation prizes." Thinking it fodder for future literary adventures, I wrote the words, along with the children's definition, a reward for losers, on the whiteboard and promptly transitioned into instructional mode.

A third of the way through the math lesson, at least five, shrill, 8 year-olds' voices sounded the alert, "Mrs. Adams, Mrs. Adams, someone is at the door! Can I let him in? Can I, can I, pleeeease?"

There, looking through the glass, stood, (dummm-dum-dum-dum-dummmmm), the Head of School, my boss's boss. Momentarily, I hesitated. But, seeing his impatient look, and the eager features of my charges, I motioned for the Helper of the Day to greet our visitor.

"Don't mind me," he announced, "I've only come to observe."

What started off as a normal day in the land of second grade education, evolved into a nightmare. I found myself flattened onto a glass slide and squeezed under the oppressive barrel of a microscope, through which the concentrated eye of another examined my imperfections.

Observe, I thought. *Observe me cascading into the conundrum of analyzing every word I say while I'm saying it. Observe me trying to gingerly release my tongue from a square knot. Observe me silently chastising myself for imperceptible errors.*

My rational alter-ego jumped to the rescue. *Just do what you normally do. You're a good teacher.*

Trying to remain calm and continue on as if the interloper sat amongst us wearing a bulbous, red clown nose and Mr. Potato Head's green glasses, I launched into an explanation of the day's exercise: Calculating the most direct route between two places on a map.

Steering the learners through workbook page 222, I solicited answers to several questions. Hands shot up. Correct responses poured from mouths like nectar from dew licked flowers.

Keep it going kids. Shine, shine, shine.

Yet, I still had to ford the difficult portion of the tutorial; guiding pupils in estimating the total kilometers of each possible route from Corncob Junction to Blueville, to find the shortest distance.

Finally, my students agreed upon two possibilities. The next step: To add a series of double-digit numbers to determine the absolute shortest course. With their guidance, I performed the addition operations on the board.

After correcting the computation of the child who walked me through the second problem, I declared, "And, so, as you can see, we should choose route A from Corncob Junction to Blueville." She nodded at me with a confused downturn of her mouth.

A hand shot up. A blond girl with pigtails excitedly bounced in her seat.

"Yes, Kelly?"

"That's not the answer I got. I got 165 km for route A and 163 km for route B."

"Well let's add again," I said, confidently.

In a teacher tone, I paced through the mathematical steps. Thank goodness I faced the whiteboard when my gut hit the floor like a stone. "Ooh! It seems Mrs. Adams made a mistake," I exclaimed, in cheap falsetto.

When at last our visitor exited, and I wriggled free from the coverslip pinning me under the magnification lens, my heart slowed and the voice of reason again spoke. *Everybody blunders. Children need to witness adults admitting errors. You demonstrated good character.*

As I breathed a deep sigh of relief, I glanced at the note on the whiteboard that I wrote to myself earlier that day. EEK!

I felt certain my boss's boss would soon award me a constellation prize of my own.

And this time my inner voice didn't even bother to talk me out of it.

Guide to Estonia

Costa Rica *(February 12th)* - All I wanted to do was flop around on my lounge chair, turning over from time to time to make sure I was evenly baked on both sides. The biggest excitement we had experienced since our plane landed was a wild Iguana creeping under my husband's chaise, turning over his drink, and stealing the cherry. And that was just fine with me.

But a Tico convinced two lazy Gringos to try an eco-tour. He recommended the night excursion out to a deserted beach to watch sea turtles lay their eggs. That evening, we, along with about 30 tourists, ranging in color from light red to bright red, gathered in a small hut by a shallow lagoon and to receive our instructions.

Thus, 30 trusting Gringos without flashlights followed five men, whose English we could barely understand, into an inky dark night. We chugged across the lagoon in a small boat with no life jackets. We walked down a desolate mile strip of beach. They herded us into a corral equipped with crude wooden benches. They left us there in the dark.

One big-mouthed, know-it-all, neighbor from the north kept the air stirred with his constant expert exhortations on our mission. He had participated the night before. He even assured one traveler, whom he accosted, wanting to know her homeland, then responding to her in Spanish once she told him, that he was well aware that Estonia is located in Europe. "We don't speak Spanish there," she admonished him and turned away.

After an hour of listening to the guy drone on like a diesel truck, and jumping to our feet every time we thought we saw a flashlight flickering in our direction, hoping this would be the moment, my husband and I decided to explore. Beyond the gate to the beach, in the middle of sandy, roadless terrain we found a bar, stcoked and open for business. Very odd in a Twilight Zone sort of way.

We walked back to the holding area. Still dark. Still no word from our "guides," whom, as the hours wore on, I began to think of as captors. We had no light, except that from the bar, and no way to leave, except to swim. Trapped. I nearly lost my mind.

Finally, Tico returned. In a thick accent he explained there were no sea turtles for us to view. We must leave. And he took off at a quick clip, back toward the boat, flashlight extinguished. By the time it registered that we were to follow, he was ahead by the length of a football field. Instead of guiding us, he did his best to disappear.

Suddenly, we bumped into the back of him, still in the pitch black. He then yelled for us to stop, turned on his flashlight, and pointed out a lone baby turtle scrambling toward the water. He must have spotted it with his infrared eyes, because there was no light from the moon. It had dipped below the horizon long before.

Our loud turtle expert in residence, the Yankee (hate to say it, but he was), dropped down on his knees and told us all to stand back. He knew what he was doing. He had attended the night prior, when they also saw no nesting turtles. Blah, blah, blah. I wanted to remind him this was an eco-tour, not an ego-tour, but my husband pinched me when I started to say it.

I wanted to tell the guy that there are no single hatchlings, that these were not the alleged nesting grounds, and that the "guide" had ditched us so he could sneak and drop that turtle out of his pocket to give us all a not so cheap thrill. I wanted to, in my sassiest voice, inform him that he had foolishly, not once, but twice, paid $40 to get dragged on a Costa Rican Snipe Hunt.

And I desperately wanted to hold up a map of Europe and have him locate Estonia on it.

Tuck in Your Skirt and Run

On the first morning of the school year, parents and students came to meet the teachers. Last minute Lucy like I am, trying to fit one more thing in before the bell rings and chugging coffee to roll back the morning fog, I rushed to the girls' restroom with mere moments to spare.

Quickly exiting the stall, I stopped to wash my hands, check my teeth, re-apply lipstick, and make a cursory inspection of my overall appearance. My head nodded in approval.

The night before, I selected my outfit very carefully, looking for something that said, I'm hip and sassy, but sophisticated and intelligent, too. I'll keep your children safe, teach them everything they need to know in second grade, and have fun doing it.

All that came in an above the knee, flouncy hemmed, black with white polka-dotted skirt paired with a three-quarter length sleeved, white, fitted blouse shirred through the bodice. Smartly beaded half-inch heels finished the ensemble.

I winked self-assuredly into the mirror at myself, complimenting my style. Making my exit into the hallway with confidence and a skip, I did the #1-teacher-walk toward my colleagues flanking the walls outside my classroom, all chit-chatting and practicing their smiles.

Shoulders back, stomach in, I strode past flashing my most intimidating *I'm-ready-for-anything* expression.

Someone screamed. Someone gasped. Someone laughed. Someone chased me into my classroom and yanked on the back of my skirt. "What?" I exclaimed.

But my fellow faculty member silently quaked, which made me start turning like a dog chasing its tail.

"You're fine, now," she squeaked out.

My friend squatted in the floor holding her sides with one arm and covering her mouth with the other hand. Then she took a deep breath to compose herself, stood, but stooped again, wracked with gut wrenching guffaws. Finally she managed to inform me, through giggles and gulps, that I boldly strutted down the hall with the hem of my skirt tucked into the back of my grannified, pink panties, which, she consoled me, plentifully covered my rear end.

I screamed. I gasped. I tried to picture if my underwear had holes or not, since I hadn't put as much effort into choosing it as I had the rest of my clothing. I laughed. I worried. "Did Mr. . . . oh my gosh . . . did Mr. . . .

ohhhh noooo. . ." I hooted. I fretted.

If my day had ended there, I possibly could have put a positive spin on it.

Yet, exhausted from the regular routine after a whole summer off, I still had to load my own children into the car and run errands. My kids immediately threw themselves into a full-fledged, inconsequential argument about pencil lead. Snapping, I threatened dire consequences to any one of them who dared say another word.

Well whoa-dang if my daughter didn't go ahead and dare. "I'm going to spank you," I promised.

Next stop, when she hopped out of the car, I turned her around and swatted her fanny.

Almost simultaneously with my forward swing, but too late to interrupt it, I heard, "Hi, Mrs. Adams," from the car next to ours, and looked up to see two students and a parent waving in my direction.

When I related this unfortunate coincidence to the other second grade teacher and told her how I stood there and dumbly smiled, unable to think what to do next, my cohort replied, through throat-closing mirth, "You should have tucked your skirt in your panties and run!"

Emergency Fashion

My Saturday shaped up to be a disaster.

Standing on the top ladder rung, the one with the warning label that says not to, I wiggled to balance the wobble. The ladder legs straddled the side of our deep porcelain tub. One leg toed its way into the drain and another faked a sturdy plant on the tub's downslope. The other two legs reached unsteadily toward the black and white tile floor near the sink.

Three fingers on my left hand held a paint cup while my thumb and index finger clung to the shower curtain rod. With my other hand, I reeeeeeeeeeached as far as I could, to dab the spot in the angle where the walls meet. Lunging back to dip my brush in the cup, I glimpsed my reflection in the bathroom mirror.

"If I fall off of this ladder," I told my husband, "brush my hair, paint my toenails, freshen my lipstick, and dress me in something cute before taking me to the emergency room or, heaven forbid, the morgue," as if a guy who claims he can't do the detail painting could pull black silk slacks over a protruding broken bone without ripping them, or slip me into my white blouse with the three-quarter length sleeves without getting head-wound blood on it.

"What's wrong with what you have on?" he asked, serious as a felony.

I weebled the ladder back toward the mirror. "Look at me! This shirt is faded, I'm splattered with paint, and my ponytail is lopsided. I can see my purple drawers through that hole in the seat of my pants."

"You look fine to me," he insisted. "But what would you recommend, should the unthinkable, but very possible in your current position, happen?"

Recalling advice I supplied my own mother, in my infinite 13 year-old wisdom, back when she was my age, I replied "Not jeans."

"But I like you in jeans," he said.

"That's what worries me."

"How about a skirt," he suggested.

"Make sure it's not too short. The black one with white polka-dots that hits at mid-knee would look great. Pair it with the shirt gathered at the bodice."

"I have no clue what you're talking about. Just trust me to make a good decision."

"You'll dress me in something that looks good to you, or, worse, something you've always wanted me to wear. There's no telling what those ER folks will think we've been up to. Not painting, that's for sure."

"Hubba-hubba," he tooted, in typical male bravado.

"No boots," I continued. "Unless they have a low-profile heel."

"Bodice? Low profile? What the?"

"Comfortable, closed-toe shoes are probably best."

"You'll be on your back," he reminded me.

"The tunnel to the light might be long," I reminded him. "There may well be a whole lot of walking in the afterlife and I sure don't want to go limping in looking like a hussy. Which brings us to undergarments."

"You want me to change your underwear?"

"Listen," I commanded. "Didn't your mother talk to you about underwear and accidents? Put me in plain, white Hanes for Her with the elastic intact." Seeing a gleam in his eye, I added, "I won't think it one bit funny if I come-to getting sawed in half by a thong."

"I tell you what," he offered, fed up with emergency fashion, "come on down off that ladder and go freshen your lipstick and put on your crisis panties. I'll finish this."

"Really?"

"Really."

Disaster averted.

Create the Ripples, Consume the Calm

I have a chivalrous husband. He runs my bath water. He pumps gas for me. He makes my coffee in the morning. He helps me with technical stuff, like the clock in my car.

"Is that the right time?" he asked me on Sunday, when he sat in my passenger seat on the way home from church.

"No, it's fast," I affirmed.

"I thought I fixed that for you," he said, thumping the face of it.

"You did," I reassured him. "But it keeps skipping ahead. It was only two minutes fast. Now it's five or six minutes fast."

"That doesn't drive you crazy?" He couldn't understand how I could tolerate the inconsistency between my watch, the stove, and my dashboard.

"No, I like when I think I'm running late for work and I get there and find out I'm early." I smiled broadly while remembering that feeling. It's like a massage therapist squeezing my neck tightly, then slowly letting go to relieve the tension; only it's a lot cheaper.

He didn't get it. "That seems like a lot of avoidable stress."

But I wouldn't know what serenity is if I didn't chuck a pebble into my placid pond now and then. I create the ripples so I can consume the calm. It's an addiction.

An addiction, very much like any other, that interferes with my normal daily functioning. On Monday, after a very long day, I stood around with other mothers waiting for our daughters to come out of ballet. One mother, making conversation, asked, "Are you having fun?"

I hadn't given it any thought. I mean, every Monday I do the same thing I did the Monday before and the one before that. And somewhere along the line, I quit wondering if I was having fun. "I don't know," I sighed in response. "I get so busy each week checking off things on my list, prioritizing to get it all done, and getting to Friday to find out I didn't get much done at all. I keep telling myself, *As soon as I finish such and such, or do this or do that, then I'm going to do something terrific.* But I never finish such and such or accomplish this or that. I'm just spinning my wheels, doing the same things over and over again. Then I flop in bed at night, exhausted, so I can get up the next morning and run in place all over again. Maybe it's fun. I don't know."

The other woman smiled pleasantly at me. "I'm sorry," she said gently, "I think you misunderstood me. I asked, 'Are you having one?'" She

politely extended a tray of cookies toward me that one of my more
counterparts had brought for the rest of us to sample. I forced a sm
accepted the offering, passing the plate on to the next lady.

Feeling incredibly conspicuous, all I wanted to do was crawl bac
my car and see my clock running 6 minutes fast so that I could feel like I'd
found time when I got home and the digits on the oven clued me in that I
had more day left than I thought.

But then, Tuesday might cure my melancholy just as well.

Book Tour in Birmingham

Neil was a seventy-one year-old curmudgeon convinced he's taking the carpool lane to hell; no exit ramps. Len was a fifty-ish agnostic-sliding-toward-atheist bent on saving Neil's soul, or at least convincing Neil it's all in his head. And me? I was an un-suspecting author conducting a book signing in a cozy book nook in Birmingham.

Sitting on a nearby sofa, they caught me eavesdropping on their private conversation - Len convincing Neil that Neil's soul is as saved as Neil believes it is. Therefore, I suppose, I deserved the heckling I duly received.

"You wrote a humor book, huh?" questioned Len redundantly.

"What's it about," groused Neil. "Say anything about George Bush?"

I shook my head.

"The pope?"

I indicated, no.

"Any dirty jokes?" As I raised my hands, palms up, and shrugged, he nonverbally expressed his deep disappointment at my perceived dismal failure in literature.

I explained, "My mama taught me three things a proper lady should never discuss at social gatherings: politics, religion, and money. And that I should take great pains never to stray into off-color language, no matter how heathenish the company [no slight meant toward my haranguers]."

"Well," Neil expounded, "how can you be funny, then?"

"Can I ask how old you are?" Len said, knowing full-well he already just did. He was bold for a boy from Auburn, Alabama. Although, I could tell from his sweater-vest his mother had raised him better than that.

I mouthed the answer, anyway.

"Oh," he exclaimed, repenting of his sinful ways, "I never would have guessed. You look much, much younger."

All offenses pardoned, I effused, "If I had a gold star, I would march right over and plant it on your forehead."

Killjoy Neil, wishing to divert the conversation back to his own nit-picking and the possibility of bogging me down in an unseemly debate, quizzed, "Been on Oprah yet?"

"No," I laughed.

No need to say more since Neil had set himself up to poke, "Oh, that's right. Oprah's on tour with Obama."

"Who would you rather see in office," quipped Len, jovially joining the attempt to corner me, "Hilary Clinton or Martha Stewart?"

"What does it matter?" Neil, thoroughly riled, unwittingly rescued me. "Not a one of 'em will do anything about the war in Iraq."

Len, the agnostic optimist soothingly said, "We can't win that war. We're a predominantly Christian country fighting a wholly Muslim country. A merciful God fighting a just God." The religion trump fully played upon the political ace, he continued, "Our forgiving God will let them all go free to aid Allah in crushing us like frogs on asphalt."

"Is that what they taught you at Auburn University?" asked Neil.

"Impugning my alma mater?" responded Len.

"Did you know that 87% of all scratch-billionaires never went to college?" segued Neil.

I couldn't help myself. "Making sure we don't overlook drawing the money card from the deck, I see."

Neil then grumbled, "I've got to go," pushing himself up from the soft sofa with a groan.

But before either man got two steps toward the door I appealed to each one's sensibilities. "Gentlemen, no disrespect, but the guilt my mother will place upon my heart for having delved into topics unfit for delicate southern flowers heavily preys on my wits. And believe me, she already senses my transgression in the marrow of her spine. I believe it's your chivalrous and bounden duty to now give her a reason to be proud of me."

They departed clutching signed books. And I know I'm on my way, now that I have hecklers.

The War on Aging

On my bookshelf, I have two books on aging. One is entitled *The Art of Growing Older* and the other *How We Die*. I have officially entered the war on aging which, from my observations, is terminal. And, inspired by my literature, I fully intend to stylishly look like death.

It has only recently come to my attention that I don't look quite so freshly hatched as I had imagined. Maybe it's denial, but until a few months ago I didn't think I looked a day over eighteen. Then, unexpectedly, I realized that either my mirror is on the blink, or I look almost a million drillion days over 35.

So, I've moved on from self-deception to self-preservation. My plan is to reduce, if not to halt, the progression of lines in my face that, in my faulty mirror, resemble fjords carved in the Swiss Alps over the last 65,000 years.

But in my quest for youth I find myself confused by all the products available and frustrated by time constraints in which to experiment with each. Do I want my face lotion to actively hydrate or intensely moisturize? Should I buy the product with alpha hydroxy acids or the one with antioxidants?

Would my evenings be better if I treated myself with an enriched night cream or with a night reform treatment? The latter sounds like it might contain a lobotomy enabling me to just forget my fine lines and wrinkles. Intriguing . . .

Designers of anti-aging products are cornering me and forcing me to decide if I want to reduce, firm, plump, exfoliate, minimize, reverse, cover-up, repair, replenish, or perfect. And every potion makes promises . . . everything from turning back the clock to granting me three wishes. A plain Jane like me has difficulty deciphering the wording on the labeling, much less understanding exactly what the substances in those beautiful jars will achieve; especially when confronted with product names like Lancome Sensation Totale-C Perfecting Complex. Perhaps what I really need is a course in cosmetic chemistry 101.

I'm learning as I go, however. Some lessons are harder than others. I have discovered the importance of not using the sea salt scrub on my hands in winter, unless I need to feel the sting of lotion applied to raw skin. Likewise, that part of the foot paddle that resembles a cheese grater . . . also feels like a cheese grater.

It is imperative that I not use the peel-off mask around small children, unless, of course, it is Halloween and I want to scare the pants off of them by removing my face right before their horror stricken eyes. My children are scheduled for a battery of therapy techniques as a result of that one miscalculation in the aging battle. Equally essential: don't leave the peel-off mask on too long; not only will my children require intervention, but I will need a skin graft.

I am hopeful that my anti-aging efforts are paying off. I felt ecstatic the day an older gentleman mistook me for a teenager. It turns out, however, that he was a ninety-five year-old Alzheimer's patient out for an illicit stroll and mistook me for his teenage daughter who is actually seventy.

But I will take what I can get.

Here's the good news. In my quest for the fountain of youth, I have found one surefire product that will take years off the face and body. It is inexpensive, simple to use and readily available. It works miracles ladies!:

A twenty-five watt lightbulb.

An Eye-Opening Experience

No matter how I try to avoid it, I eventually end up grocery shopping at Wally World, more an experience than a place, on a Friday night.

When I pass through the automatic doors, I feel grotesquely transformed into a mama wearing undersized spandex shorts and an oversized T-shirt, who before entering stomped out a cigarette with a bedroom-slippered foot, screeching, "You kids better git yer butts over here! I said shut-up!" I always feel uneasy, like something important is missing; maybe my lipstick, or a baby dressed only in a disposable diaper.

It ain't pretty.

When that inevitable Friday night arrived, I cursed my fortunes and railed against the necessities of life. As I entered the packed parking lot, however, I resolved to make the most of things and keep my conduit open for story lines.

First thing, while grabbing dog food, I overheard a wizened woman speaking to a young lady with a newborn.

"Ooh, let me see that baby, chile," the older lady said. "That a pretty baby. How old she be?"

"Fo weeks," replied the new mother.

"What you callin' her," the grandmotherly woman inquired.

"Shauntantaniqua, but we say Tanika."

"You can spell that?"

"Yeah."

"As long as you can spell it, girl, you alright," said the matron.

I went to the dairy section, thinking, I bet I couldn't spell it the same way twice.

Many aisles later, believing the story-well dry, I picked through produce. Two aged men sharing a grocery list approached. They weaved to and from each other gathering items. One ended up by me.

His friend drew near and exclaimed, "What are you doing?"

"The list said red apples. I'm getting apples," the man next to me gruffed.

"Those ain't apples, you old fool. You've got tomatoes in that bag."

Tickled by this exchange, I let a giggle slip, which turned the mistaken man's ire on me. "That's not funny," he growled. "I cain't see worth a dern. You laughing at the handicapped."

I blushed from the knees up and immediately steered my buggy toward the check-out lane; a bottle neck of children crying, noses running, ice cream melting, and parents giving "butt whoopins." I coached myself that if I could squeeze through that narrow passage of torment with my sensibilities and bread still fluffy, I would make it.

But broken by Wally World, I dragged my squished sensibilities to my car and started putting flattened bread into the rear. A deep male voice from behind asked, "Ma'am, can I help you?"

Of course, being a female alone in a parking lot on a Friday night, I felt threatened. "No. I've got it," I tersely assured the young man dressed in a white oxford, black tie, and dark pants.

"Let me explain how you can spend eternity in paradise with your family," he persisted.

"What? You know how I can dodge coming here on a Friday night?" I retorted with sarcasm. Noting my resistance to his ill-conceived method of message spreading, he tucked tail.

Then, as I rounded the side of my minivan, a wiry, weathered man smoking a cigar sat on the bumper of the auto next to mine. "Yes, ma'am," he addressed me in a bluesy voice. "I jest prays for 'em all. That's right. I jest prays fer 'em all. Amen."

"That's nice," I hastily affirmed.

"C'mone back here," he invited. "I needs to talks to you."

At that juncture I decided I would not conduct anymore research at Wally World. I best stick to bike shorts, bedroom shoes, and blending in.

Stinky Feet

Painfully shy as a child, I've retained some of that self-consciousness as an adult. In my abnormal psychology class in college, after comparing myself to the symptoms listed in each textbook chapter, I expected my professor at any time to call me forward as an example of every mental disorder examined in the text. I, as well as everyone else, could clearly see I had paranoid schizophrenic bipolar antisocial personality disorder accompanied by delusional thinking and exacerbated by adult onset ADD.

Once the quarter ended, I reverted back to a normal, healthy co-ed, fearing regular things like bad guys and cancer. But, due to my insecurities that have plagued me since my youth, I still sometimes think people are talking about me:

"Hey, you seen Shaquita?" said cashier Number 1.

"Naw, I ain't seen her. What she do?" responded cashier Number 2.

"Girl, you know Shaquita, she always up to something," replied Number 1.

"Yeah, but her feet stink," supplied Number 2.

"Uh-huh. They do. Her feet stink like a man's feet," affirmed Number 1.

"They stink like an athletic man's feet," added Number 2.

"Somebody ought to tell her her feet stink. She need to go see a doctor about that."

"I'm glad my feet don't stink like no man's."

"You got that right. I don't want no stinky man's feet. That nasty."

I walked to my car worried about my foot odor. What else could have triggered such an odd conversation except somebody's smelly feet. Maybe everyone but me could smell my feet. Maybe I had grown desensitized to the odor. There you have it, I decided, my feet stink like a man's. I am Shaquita.

By the time I got home to my comfort zone, I had talked myself out of believing they had a coded dialogue just to make fun of me. But I did put on closed-toe shoes to wear to a party later that evening.

At the party I couldn't figure out how to use the bottle opener. I turned my un-opened beverage all which-a-way, but it didn't make sense to me that I had to turn my bottle upside down to open it. All the liquid would spill out when I pried off the cap.

Seeing my struggle, a friend walked over and said, "This is how you use it. You have to pick it up and hold it like this." He took the bottle from my hand and demonstrated.

I nodded, feeling silly, wondering how close a person his height had to stand to detect foot odor. He's not a tall guy.

"But next time," he continued, "you could twist off the top."

"I can? It doesn't have those little arrows on it."

The way he looked at me when I uttered those words made me wish I could reel them back in. Instead, I cast out another line, saying, "I must be having a blond moment."

To this statement, a woman standing with us commented, "I bet I have more of those than you."

Oh no, I thought, is it that obvious? "I know. I've got roots. They look awful, I'm sure. I really need to make an appointment with my hairdresser. He does a good job. I haven't had time to get my hair done lately. Growing up I always had blond hair, and I couldn't let go of it when it started turning dark."

The more I talked the more her face clouded with consternation. My bottle-opener friend said to her, "Your hair isn't really that color is it?"

"No," she smiled, "This is Tawny Velvet from a box."

She looked directly at me, concern and sympathy swinging from her lips like a wrecking ball. "I meant you seem so smart, being a writer and all, that you probably have very few blond moments. But, well, um, . . .," she trailed off.

Good grief. I knew it all along. I really do have paranoid schizophrenic bipolar antisocial personality disorder accompanied by delusional thinking and exacerbated by adult onset ADD. And my feet stink, too.

That's Life

Waves licked my toes again and again, threatening to wash me and my chair out to sea. Each time they thought they had me beat, I dragged my seat a few inches inland, book in tow.

That's when I first spotted her, wearing a black, one-piece bathing suit with seams audibly moaning from the pressure of dammed flesh. She bobbed effortlessly in the ocean, up and down, rising and falling with the swells, buoyed by her bulk. Even as the incoming tide grew more aggressive, pushing at her waist on the way in and grabbing at her ankles on the way out, her enormous torso bulged steady above the water.

What force of nature, after all, could move a woman whose companions had to remove one wall of her house and fork-lift her into the back of a pick-up truck to haul her to the beach?

Sharks disregarded her thighs, not wishing to start something they couldn't finish.

I averted my gaze and forced my ogling eyes to find my place on the page. Yet, unable to resist, I peered over the binding of my novel to watch, amazed, as she bounced and hopped, pushed a little shallower every time.

Unexpectedly, a gi-normous breaker hit her from behind, knocking her down, and rolling her up the beach like a helpless jelly fish.

Her two female friends went howling after her. The wild surf, in its mercy, released its victim back to them. But, alas, just as they reached her, the sea heaved her up the beach again.

Dropping my literature, I gawked at the two people grappling their portly compatriot, who thrashed about in vain, attempting to right herself by gripping loose sand in her chubby fingers. White foam lugged her away.

The ocean labored to either cough her out like a ball of phlegm, or swallow her up like gristle on a slab of steak, but it couldn't make headway with either. So it relentlessly rocked her from front to back in ankle deep water. And every time she could get what looked like an elbow under her, the sea returned to rub her face in it.

The other two women, one on her knees pushing from behind, one standing and pulling from above, proved no match for the power of Poseidon. Slippery sunscreen paired with a body they couldn't wrap their towels around, made saving efforts lack effectiveness and grace.

Another misstep and they all lay in a heap of unwieldy flesh, undulating with the whims of the waves.

I got so convulsively tickled that the sand around my chair cracked. Rivulets of tears streaked down my cheeks. The trio looked up and caught me laughing.

In the throes of my guttural gyrations, sudden guilt struck my heart. People of my size and stature have no business finding humor at the expense of the overly weighty. And, political correctness aside, as my mama would point out, I know better. She raised me right.

I tried to stifle my giggles, but my body shook like a bed in a New Jersey hotel room with a fresh quarter in the slot. A cavern opened around my chair. *I'm on the short track to Hell*, I scolded myself.

Nevertheless, the women's countenances softened and betrayed their own mirth. Each time they managed to get their faces above water, they themselves found the situation nothing short of hilarious.

Sink, swim, or ride the wave. And when you can't do that, giggle. I thought to myself, *That's life*.

I only hope I can laugh, or even better, make other people chuckle, when I'm on my belly wallowing in it.

Flight Plan

An old southern proverb says a belle should always have two things when taking flight, metaphorically, metaphysically, or mechanically: A plan, and clean underwear in case the plan doesn't work out. Much to my mama's and my husband's chagrin, I place little emphasis on plans. And I shy away from communal examination of my foundation garments. Neither stops me, however, from taking flight:

"And heck," I said, behaving as if I had a real proposal my husband couldn't help but embrace, "if we're going all the way to Shreveport, we may as well go on over to Texas." I just threw in the Texas thing to give him something to say "No" to, thus softening the inevitable consequences of saying "Yes" to my first crazy impulse.

Like my husband, and my mama before him, the Delta ticket agent at counter #80 tisk-tisked my desire to fly by the seat of my pants. "You're too late to check your bags," she informed us, taking absurd delight in being the bearer of bad news. "You'll have to carry them on." Her long, bony, red-tipped finger pointed toward the black trash-compactor. "Discard your shampoo."

As I dropped $75 of toiletries into the trashcan, I could swear she called after me, "Your shampoo and your little dog, too, my pretty. Eeeeeeeeeeee, heeee, heeeee, heeeee."

Only minutes remaining until our plane taxied down the runway, we hurried toward security, disrobed, and placed our shoes, belts, and dignity into plastic slop buckets for strangers to rummage through and scrutinize. My purse and suitcase traveled behind on the conveyor belt.

On the other side of the metal detector, a perturbed security agent squawked, "Whose is this?" Looking down, ignoring the question, I observed all the nekkid feet parading around and made a mental note to modernize the proverb to also include crisp socks and a pedicure.

"People, pay attention. Whose is this?" She held up toothpaste, face cleanser, and other contraband.

Recognizing the items, I weakly acknowledged, "Mine," hoping the officer appreciated that my underwear was clean when she plundered through my suitcase.

"I'm throwing it away," she tersely admonished.

Grossly violated but not yet intimidated, I pleaded, "My deodorant too? But it's a solid."

"Sorry, ma'am."

She wasn't.

"But it *is* a solid," I desperately insisted.

"Keep moving," someone barked. Out of options and arguments, I gathered together my belongings and my crumpled spirit. Tears welled up from deep inside.

The stress getting to him, too, or he never would have said it, my husband asked, "Why are you crying? It's just deodorant."

"Leave me alone," I whispered, choking back sobs.

It wasn't JUST deodorant. It wasn't even about the deodorant. It was about my ill-preparedness exposed to the world. It was about strange, soiled hands pawing through my clean underwear. And now that he had pointed it out, it was about making a public spectacle of myself.

Boarding the plane with seconds to spare, a recollection of my great-Aunt Mary West struck me. *Remembah who you ahr and whe-ah you come from*, she's always advised those of us who strike out on adventure.

I sucked in my stomach, dried my eyes, and minded my posture. Although stripped of my apparent thinly veiled plan to hijack an aircraft using solid Secret deodorant and in dire need of a laundromat to freshen my unmentionables, I still had my lipstick; and a girl who has her lipstick has everything she needs.

Inspired by another little southern proverb - *When the pieces fall apart, put some color on and pull yourself togethah* – I took flight.

Chapter Two

Weaving a Tangled Web

My sister-in-law's husband, a typical male, considers eating out a competition with the chef. Not only does he state, "I feel defeated if I don't eat my whole meal in one sitting," but he also gets frustrated with his wife who eats half in the restaurant and, without exception, takes the other half home in a Styrofoam box.

She defends herself to her husband, saying, "I like to take the leftovers to work for lunch. I get two meals for the price of one." Girls don't gorge, they economize. It's how we justify purchasing our purses and shoes.

Walking and Smoking and Other Faux Pas

My grandmother, God rest her soul, defined herself as a southern lady. I really should capitalize the "S" in southern and "L" in lady, because she'll roll over in her grave when she finds out that I didn't.

We called her Mama T, and she could recite her heritage back to the American Revolution, or to Adam and Eve, depending on the patience of the listener.

I lacked the fortitude to sit through one of her lectures on lineage. What did capture my attention, however, were Mama T's unspoken, but vigorously adhered to, rules of ladylike behavior.

For example, a lady might smoke. And she definitely knows how to walk with just the right amount of swing in her hips. But she never, ever smokes and walks. According to my grandmother, "That's common."

I, conversely, think it's because running out of breath strolling to the grocery store entrance, and hacking like a lung will rupture, detracts from a lady's aura.

A southern lady, too, must willingly suffer for beauty. If you have ever worn a pair of shoes that bore holes through your feet for the sake of looking "put together," or had your mother pull your tresses into a bun so tightly that it felt like your brain might burst through your hair follicles, then I need not explain.

A belle knows her fashion. Mama T kept her white shoes tucked safely in the closet from the Tuesday following Labor Day until Easter; whether Easter came in mid-March or not until a sweltering Sunday in April. And the Holiest of days did not **pass** without her togged up in those white shoes, and a hat, even if the temperature dropped to twenty-eight degrees, and it snowed.

She put on that sleeveless pink dress, too.

A lady never wears red, black or white to a wedding, or white, red or fuscia to a funeral. She would not blatantly disrespect brides and widows by drawing attention to herself. I am of the opinion, nonetheless, that brides remain too self-absorbed, and widows too inconsolable, to notice what little ol' me wore to the occasion.

But, we wouldn't want people to talk, now, would we?

Speaking of gossip, Mama T knew the proper way to prudently call attention to indiscretions. It pained her to mention other's errors out loud; so much so, that she spoke of them only in thunderous whispers, which could carry across three church pews during a robust rendition of Amazing Grace by the entire flock of the Mount Bethel Southern Baptist Congregational Church.

Yet, without exception, a girl of proper rearing knows when to talk and when to remain silent. Ladies might quietly gab about faux pas, but they never talk politics, religion or money in mixed company; unless, of course, the company brought mixers. But, just because she doesn't converse on these subjects doesn't mean that a lady shouldn't look like she's on the winning wing, she's one of the chosen, and she's got it to burn.

And ladies' clubs, such as my grandmother's Sew 'n' Sews, serve as the proving grounds. I chanced to accompany Mama T to a club meeting once; no one pulled out handwork. They brought wine, deviled eggs, homemade pimento cheese finger sandwiches and pictures of their granddaughters' debutante balls.

In short, a woman with manners never reveals her own secrets, always gives "proper" kisses, loves her cousins, knows her pedigree, and remembers the South. And Mama T's life illustrated that a girl can have as much fun as she wants, so long as she conducts herself like a lady.

Elder Rage

My grandfather doesn't speed, unless he's late; he doesn't drink, unless it's vodka at a Russian Orthodox wedding; he doesn't shop, unless he's watching QVC; he doesn't give money to telemarketers, unless the representatives ask nicely; he doesn't read his junk mail, unless he has time (and he always has time); he doesn't go to church, unless it's downhill; and he doesn't cuss, unless my aunt demands that he hand over his car keys and checkbook.

When that happened, the cussing I mean, my aunt went to the bookstore and purchased a volume on elder rage. She evidently thought it odd that a grown man, who raised her to adulthood, would feel anger at the stripping of his independence. Unexpectedly, he refused to climb on the ice floe like a responsible senior citizen and let his children shove him out to the offshore glue factory.

In the midst of all this activity it dawned on me that I'll reach that point in life too, when my children decide that my idiosyncrasies suddenly indicate a decline into senility.

My brood will get in cahoots and come to the unanimous decision that I am too short to drive. Yet, no one exhibited fear when I drove him to soccer, cub scouts, ballet, Florida, Tennessee and further looking over the dashboard through the steering wheel to see the road. What's so different if I'm doing it when I have blue hair and I'm eighty?

If I'm thirty-five and I put the ice cream in the refrigerator and the milk in the pantry, I clean up the mess and we all laugh. If I'm seventy-five, I clean up the mess while my children quietly conference on how to have me declared incompetent. Somehow, the incident will signify that I am throwing their inheritance out the window as I speed down the interstate at twenty miles per hour, with my right blinker on, at two o'clock in the afternoon, trying to make it home before dusk.

Forty years from now, the same absent-minded errors I make during the naiveté of their youth will incriminate me as feeble-minded: toting my purse around the house because I forgot it dangled on my shoulder, frantically looking for my glasses propped on my head, driving to one place when I intended to go to another, and going to the grocery store only to forget what I needed.

If my mob looked at me today with the same eyes they will see me through when I am ninety, I would already live in an Alzheimer's lockdown unit. Making pancakes for dinner would demonstrate that I am disoriented to time and place. Confusedly identifying them by each others' names would cause them to conclude that I don't recognize them anymore. Buying cabbage instead of X-box games would point to my mishandling of finances. Telling them to clean their rooms before bedtime would classify as sundowner syndrome.

When my kids retire and begin to sniff out my mothball trail, I may gather up my cats and change the locks. I'll have the last laugh while I "run away" on my walker. My heirs will dig for those jars of pennies they think I foolishly buried in the backyard; an ill-fated attempt to rescue me from my alleged peculiarities when I'm ninety-five, and shake me down for a little of the money they think I should have given them when they were twenty. But, I will have already donated the pennies, all 10,000,000,000 of them, to that nice gentleman collecting for the charity to save the greater pygmy whooping rat of Kenya.

Who's cussing now?

The Price of Slaw in Georgia

My mother and I approached the crooked little hut with apprehension. It bore a lopsided sign painted with the letters BBQ, and the phrase Best Butts on the Beach.

On the wall next to the place-your-order-here window, the edges of a paper menu fluttered in the afternoon breeze. "Side items. Potato salad, chips, baked beans, slaw, Mama's Brunswick stew . . ." read my mother, aloud. "I wonder what they mean by Brunswick stew? Some places confuse hash with stew."

Deeply engrossed in our philosophical conversation teasing out the nuances of stew and hash, we startled when the glass window slid open and two hands reached through, dispensing tester cups. We cautiously accepted them.

Like professional tasters we held the substance up to the sunlight to ascertain thickness and consistency. We passed the samples under our noses to gauge spice and seasoning. Finding everything, thus far, agreeable, we opened our mouths and tossed back the contents like bar flies on nickel shooter night at Papa Joe's.

Brunswick stew, we both agreed.

Someone pushed the window ajar again.

"Y'all like Mama's Brunswick stew," a husky voice from within half-asked, half-stated.

"Yes," replied my mother, "but who's Mama?"

The gravelly voice put its face in the communication gap. "Who do you think?"

Fiddler crab scuttles filled the silence.

"You'll have my stew," she ordered, writing on her pad.

Watching the way her pudgy fingers gripped a pen under the strain of her bosoms resting heavily on her forearms, we naturally mumbled, "Yes ma'am."

Mama's aura caught our attention like the bearded fat lady in a red string bikini at the county fair. Her biceps bulged as much as her upper-arm under-skin sagged and swayed. Mousy hair curling from under her hairnet glistened with sweat beads. The mustache on her upper lip mesmerized us.

"What else?"

We ordered sandwich baskets. "Can I get slaw on my sandwich," my mother requested.

"Cost ya' extra," growled Mama.

"Oh, I'm from Tennessee," offered my mother.

"What's that got to do with the price of slaw in Georgia," cursed Mama.

I pondered the same thing myself, suspecting my mother of pulling a Mama T. At this juncture, I feared for the unsanitary handling of my food, as well.

Mama T, my maternal grandmother, now passed on to other audiences, often, at odd times, to total strangers, established her identity by enunciating, in her formal southern drawl, "I'm Fredda Beaton, here visiting from Memphis. I'm a member of the UDC and the DAR. My family's ancestral men fought valiantly wearing full regalia in both wars for independence. This is my daughter. She married an attorney. They live in a lovely home and drive a fine automobile . . ."

Fortunately, my mother, seeing the stricken looks on Mama's face and mine pulled up short of recounting her lineage and disclosing my social security number. She simply asked, "How much extra for the slaw?"

"Fifty cents," said Mama, slamming the portal.

My mother faced me, rattled. "I only meant to explain that in Tennessee folks eat Bar-B-Que with slaw."

"Oh," I said. "I expected you to elucidate on how you and your Cousin Jimmy took that flogging rooster on the bus to Aint Carrie's farm in Mississippi. And how she sent y'all home with it two days later, so your daddy let it go in an alley off Beale street. And how afterwards you all went to the Rendezvous for slaw on Bar-B-Que sandwiches."

She gave me the look, and countered, "What's that got to do with the price of slaw in Georgia?"

Exactly.

Big Dee

He's my daddy, but we call him "Dee," for short. Growing up, all of our friends called him Dee. Now he's Big Dee to his grandchildren. And his moniker of affection sets him apart from other fathers.

So, too, do all of his eccentricities.

Dee is a connoisseur and collector of coolers, believing no man can own too many.

He has eaten and analyzed the wares of every Bar-B-Que establishment from Miami to Montana, and has culled his acquired knowledge into a recipe for the finest pork Bar-B-Que this side of Siam.

If creeping with a gimpy limp were an Olympic sport, my daddy would be everlastingly bent from wearing his gold medals.

He drives death defyingly s-l-o-o-o-w-w-w-w. When riding with him, the hair on the back of my neck stays permanently prickled at the sensation of vehicles rushing up from behind and skirting around my father's car, barely leaving the last centimeter of compressed air undisturbed.

He knows a thousand "shortcuts," each one significantly longer than the last. He can go to the grocery store, five minutes from his house, to buy a gallon of milk, and not return home until we're all convinced he's suffered a psychogenic fugue.

In my youth, I always jumped at the chance to sidekick with my daddy, because all shortcuts eventually led to the 7-Eleven. It didn't bother me that he said nothing beyond, "Want a coke?".

My gregarious husband on the other hand completely misinterpreted the ways of Dee. Pre-betrothal, he spent six solid hours of stunning silence on a Saturday alone with my daddy. All my father said to him the entire day was, "Look in that cooler and get us a beer." Dee didn't even answer when my husband inquired, "Which cooler?"

A man of few words, Dee didn't intentionally intimidate him. My daddy drove me 30 minutes to school every morning for 3 ½ years with less than five words passing between us in all that time.

On family road trips, just as randomly as he whisked the switch from over the visor, he spontaneously stopped at places like Ron Jon's Surf Shop, Gatorland, or Ruby Falls and let us run amuck.

An alumnus of the University of Georgia, he got me hooked on all things red and black. I said, "Go Dawgs," before I said, "Dee."

He taught me to respect Mississippi, because, according to my father, whether the Federal government admits it or not, Mississippi never rejoined the Union.

A man of extremes, he wishes to retire to either coastal Maine or a Caribbean island and answer Mother Ocean's call at whichever one he chooses. Yet his mechanical abilities suit him more for a paddleboat than a powerboat.

When it comes to handyman projects, my daddy does them right the second or third time, or never. While some carpentry-challenged men break a foot and buy a new toe, my daddy breaks a foot, buys an elbow and tries to modify it with bubble gum and duct tape.

He enjoys his Scotch.
He loves my mama.
He tolerates us kids.
He believes in the merits of suffering.

As a junior in college, I called Dee to ask if I could drop an elective involving busywork that interfered with my social life. I thought I could sell it to him easier than my mama. But he said, "No." Paris Island built his character; missing a few band parties would build mine.

He's the smartest, wisest man I know; entirely cerebral.

As an attorney, clever. As a judge, merciful. As a father, sacrificial.

And I am thankful he was set aside from other fathers, reserved especially for me and my siblings.

Penelope's Curse

Midtown Memphis, July, 1951 - Six year-old, curly-headed, straw-berry blond Jane pedaled her bike over to seven year-old, lengthy-locked, golden-haired Penelope's backyard, where five goldfish swam in useless circles in a concrete pond.

Penelope, away on a visit of mercy, had left her backyard and fish-pond unattended. Jane arrived on the scene hot, sweaty, and bored.

Dipping her feet in the refreshing pond water, Jane made a quick, yet fateful, arguably pivotal, decision. Giggling and splashing and cooling considerably in the process, she caught the swimmers, one by one, and deposited them over the neighbor's fence. Then she eased into the small pool, where she spread her arms, closed her eyes, and floated, hair stream-ing like a watery blaze.

When a shadow fell across her, she opened her eyes. A hazy, haloed figure blocked the circle of sun except for the very rim. The apparition, wearing a white dress, looked down at her. Heat rippled from the ground. Angels, she thought, angels watching over me.

"Get out of that fishpond right now!" screamed the angels.

Jane sat up, her soaked hair revealing its hidden length, her blue t-shirt clinging to her ribs. The angels hadn't come for her, Penelope had; fresh from The Charitable Sisters of The Cross Home for the Aged, Infirm, and Inconsolable, where Penelope spent the morning reciting Bible verses from memory to the elderly, and all the sisters remarked favorably on Penelope's soul.

"Where are my fish," screeched Penelope. "I had five." And she listed off their names and identifying characteristics. She ran around the sides of the pond, peering into the shallows.

Jane rose. Water droplets ran down her skinny legs and over her knobby knees. She gathered up her shoes and pointed toward the fence. Penelope briskly strode in that direction searching the grass. As Jane pushed up the bike's kickstand with her toe and prepared to swing her leg over, Penelope made the gruesome discovery.

"How could you?" bawled a broken-hearted Penelope. "How could you?" she repeated. "They suffered."

A pang of guilt stabbed at Jane, now sitting on her bike, feeling her breath go short; the moisture evaporating from her skin in the broiling Memphis heat. For the first time the whole day, she thought about how the evicted fish had gasped and perished as she wallowed pleasurably in their evacuated puddle. She shrugged, just barely, but enough for the sharp-witted Penelope to notice.

Penelope took it to indicate a lack of Christian conscience, particularly since Jane had yet to utter one word of apology – one word, period – sitting on her bicycle with that dumb, helpless expression on her face. "God will punish you for this," Penelope hissed.

Jane surmised that perhaps Penelope was one of those omen-bearing angels. So she immediately sped away on her two-wheeler, toward home, the tight rings of fire returning to her hair. Penelope, in her Sunday best, cradled the victims' bodies in her palms. For good measure, she cried again, "God will punish you!"

For fifty-seven years, Jane has lived a life of penance and suffering, vacationing in Minnesota in January and forgoing air-conditioning in Georgia in August. She has waited these many years for God to exact His punishment, or to give some clear sign that He already did.

I hope He gets it over with before the angels return. I have inherited many things from Sandra Jane, like her curly mane, her knobby knees, her love of pools. I do not wish to inherit the obligatory penance and suffering or nagging agony of Penelope's unforgiving curse, as well.

Women Go and Women Come

My long-widowed uncle recently had the misfortune of needing a female to come back into his life. Post-surgery, as badly as he wanted to, he simply couldn't care for himself. Thus he suffered the benevolence of not one woman, but two sisters-in-law.

My mother and aunt competently bustled in to provide order and aid. First things first, they planned a menu and wrote a list and hurried out to stock the cupboards with nutritious foods not fit for a bachelor.

Efficiently, they shopped aisle by aisle. As the cart grew weightier, they began parking it and lighting out on hunting-gathering expeditions, returning provisions to the containment area. "Cheese," read my mother, from the list, and the women waltzed to the cold case and collected cheddar. They dropped it into a buggy, barely missing the bread.

"We've got everything," said Aunt Pat, checking the list, and they pushed the buggy to check-out lane #7. Aunt Pat unloaded each item. The checker scanned each item. My mother bagged each item. Just as Aunt Pat accepted the receipt, my mama held up a tub of cottage cheese and asked if my aunt meant to buy it.

"No," Aunt Pat replied, "did you get those Fritos?"

"Uh-uh." My mother took a closer look. "Ooh," she gasped. "Why did we buy Twinkies?" She let out another, "Ooooooh," adding, "We've got someone else's cart." Reality registered. "We've got someone else's groceries!"

They began backing into the check-out lane, attempting to make a return, chattering to the cashier that they didn't mean to do this, that they bought groceries that didn't belong to them, and questioned whether they had done something akin to stealing. A speechless clerk continued to scan the products of the person next in line, all the while keeping an eye on the two babbling customers holding up canned goods, scouring a list, and shaking their heads.

My mother decided to go find their buggy. Systematically, she strode up and down the tiled aisles. By the pasta, right where they had left it, she now recalled, was their cart, which she pushed back to check-out lane #7. And the confused cashier scanned a second basket of groceries for the two women, who watched hawkishly to make sure it was indeed filled with their hand-selected items.

While my mama and Aunt Pat struggled through the check-out lane with the two shopping carts, in the Piggly Wiggly meat section Merle reached behind him to put a package of bologna in his basket. The bologna slapped the floor, causing Ladonna to look up from the sliced turkey and fuss, "Where's our buggy?"

"I don't know," claimed Merle. "It was here just a minute ago. Then I turned around and, thhblisst, it wuz gone!"

"That ain't funny, Merle," Ladonna snorted.

"It's true," Merle insisted, spying into a passing shopper's basket to see if it contained his Twinkies and Fritos. "Ever since you done took that Mensa test on-line, you been so gol-darn uppity, with yer cottage cheese and all."

"Well, I ain't never misplaced a full-dang shopping cart in the cold cases, now, have I?" Ladonna shouted.

Ladonna stomped off muttering how she was sick and tired of Merle doing stupid stuff like this and how she was plumb fed up with his antics and she was going to the car. She huffed right past my mother and Aunt Pat wrasslin' hijacked chips and cottage cheese into the trunk of their car. Having taken care of Merle, they had to get home to concentrate their attentions on my uncle.

Summer Doldrums

Somewhere between July 4th and the dog days, summer doldrums set in. Too hot to play baseball, too hot to fish, too hot to swim, too hot to act happy, too hot to even work up a good argument. That's when my mother would shake her head at my older brother and me and serve us lectures in idleness. That's when we would flop on the front porch, sulking and thinking. That's when trouble usually started.

"What do you think would happen if you put a bullet on the train tracks," my brother would wonder out loud.

"I don't know. You got one?" I hopefully inquired.

"Nah." Then we sat a while longer soaking in that disappointment.

"How long do you think it would take us to walk from here to Atlanta?" he tried again.

"Couple days, maybe. Glad I didn't live in the olden times. 'Cause it's surely too hot to do that." Then I took my turn with the questions. "Want to pull the wings off a fly?"

"Sure."

We got up the energy to corner a fly against the screen. My brother held the body and plucked one wing from it then put the buzzing insect down on the floor. We crouched on our knees, watching the futile spinning and shaking. Now and then, when it settled down and resigned itself to doom, one or the other of us flicked it to get it going again. Sick entertainment, but entertainment nonetheless.

Losing interest, we disposed of the body in the yard and returned to flopping and sulking.

My brother broke the thick air, saying, "Think it's true that a cat always lands on its feet?"

About that time our fat, gray cat strolled by outside, without a care in the world. I looked at my brother. He looked at me. Moments later we stood at the steps sweetly calling, "Here, kitty kitty." Of course, the feline trustingly padded over and rubbed against our shins.

My brother picked her up and held her legs in his hands, her back parallel to the earth. He let go. She landed on feet, stood for a second with a stunned expression, then ran toward the back of the house.

The same time the next week, we sat around debating whether or not Tattoo from Fantasy Island had a speech impediment or talked like that because he was little. Again the cat came poking by, unaware of us. My brother said, "Once isn't always."

"Here, kitty kitty." Transgressions forgotten, she huddled next to our ankles and purred.

My brother picked her up and announced, "We're going to the hayloft." Despite the heat, in our excitement, we actually ran to the barn and climbed the ladder, squirming cat in tow, to the humid, sticky loft.

Standing at the open doors looking down on a thin layer of strewn hay, we nodded at each other. The cat sensed danger and twisted and yowled, but my comrade in mad science held tight. Gripping her front and back legs together in pairs, he held her out over the nothingness. "Ten, nine, eight, seven . . .," we counted, suspense mounting.

"Whoo-hoo!" We high-fived each other, as the feline hit the ground on all-fours and skidded off into the woods at record speed.

Another week passed, steamier than the last, and our moping and sweating seemed to have no end. That's when the cat, missing since we last spent time with her, showed up again. "I've got an idea," said my genius brother. And he ran inside.

Meanwhile, I sat very still and unthreatening, as the cat now behaved quite timidly toward me. Shortly, my brother came back out with a paper grocery bag and a gleam in his eye. I coaxed the cat over and before she knew it we had her again, headed for the hayloft.

This time I held open the grocery bag while he lowered her in, upside down. Cat wrangling ain't easy. A person never heard such hissing and spitting as we had to endure, but finally we got her secured in the bag, feet to the sky.

Holding the bundle in empty space, we shouted, "All engines are go. Blast off," and released it.

Another few days or so passed. Our elation over our experimentation fading, our mother asked, "Have y'all seen the cat, lately?"

We weren't about to let that cat out of the bag.

The Price of Building Confidence

In a diner in Northport, thumbing through The Crimson White, the University of Alabama newspaper, while enjoying my breakfast of biscuits smothered in sawmill gravy, an ad caught my attention.

I read it aloud to my sister: "Will pay $300 to girls to shave their heads."

My sister kept chewing her sausage, unfazed. "So," she flatly said. Living in a college town numbs her to the nuances of absurdity.

"Well, why do you think someone wants to pay me to shave my head," I asked.

My sister laughed. "No one wants to pay *you*," she quipped. "Someone wants to pay cute, young, co-eds who need a few bucks to make it to the end of the semester."

I ignored her intimation about my age and finances. "I think it will take a little more than that. I don't see any girl doing it for $300."

Without giving my sibling a chance to point out any other reasons why I'm not qualified to have my head shaved, I dialed the number at the bottom of the ad and left a voicemail message for whatever deranged fetishist held a pair of fantasy clippers on the other end. Then, I tore out the ad and placed it in my purse.

A short while later my cell phone rang. "Hello?"

A male voice inquired if I had called him earlier about the head shaving ad.

"Yes, I did. Why exactly do you want to pay women to shave their heads," I asked, getting right to the root of the matter. My sister looked at me and rolled her eyes. I put my finger over the receiver and whispered to her, "Be quiet. This is research for a column."

The voice on the other end replied, "I'm working up an advertising pitch. It's a one time deal [Obviously!]. I need women to let me take pictures of them before, during, and after shaving their heads."

"I don't know if I can do it for only $300; especially since it won't really mean any publicity for me."

Sounding a little desperate, he inquired, "How much do you need?"

"At least $500, maybe seven," I shot back.

"I've got some girls who say they're willing to do it for three," he retorted. But then he asked me a series of questions about my age, hair color, length, thickness, texture and so forth. My sister mouthed at me, "He's a pervert."

As for myself, I mulled over the words of my friend Charlotte: "Baldness increases a man's self-confidence. A bald man faces the daily social obstacle of overcoming the uncomfortable sensation of everyone staring at his head. A bald man, out of necessity, possesses poise under pressure."

If baldness can do that for a man, what could it do for a woman like me, I wondered? The mystery voice inside my cell phone interrupted my reverie. "Listen," he said, "let me talk to the other girls and think on it. I'll get back to you if I can use you."

I disappointedly pressed the red END button. I'd had a string of disappointments and rejections, and now it seems, I had to cope with the fact that I'm not even competent enough to have my head shaved. My sister looked at me and said, "You're a lunatic. Did you ask him what you have to wear, if anything, while he shaves your head?"

Self-assuredly, I report that I have forgiven my sister for her lack of vision, and that, as you can see, the guy called back. Confidence came at a higher price than I expected.

Seller Beware

Back in his high school heyday, my youngest brother owned a 1972 VW van, which he personally painted in psychedelic funk. Everyday, he drove to eleventh grade assembly looking like he might make an abrupt u-turn to follow the Grateful Dead instead.

Suffice it to say he never lost his ride in a mall parking lot.

Maturity, however, brought a need for reliable, not colorful, transportation, and he sold the van in an eBay auction. But the fellow who purchased it, some odd years ago, recently managed to misplace the masterpiece in Auburn, Georgia.

Last Thursday the State of Georgia notified my brother by letter that the DOT had impounded his automobile. He looked out his kitchen window. His Jeep was parked in the driveway.

Confused, he called the DOT to inquire about the purported vehicle and his specific connection to it. The paperclip pusher on the other end described the van, and my sibling sentimentally acknowledged previous ownership.

"You, sir, are the current owner. You, in fact, are the only owner of record," said the bored state employee, exasperatedly.

"Ma'am," my brother retorted, a bit too mulish for his own good, "I wasn't even born until 1981."

She snorted and gave him his options: a) pay the abandoned vehicle fine or b) pay the daily impoundment charge. All fees, fines and crimes associated with the car remained his responsibility, but, she assured him, he could not retrieve the auto, because, as he just explained to her, he had sold it.

What?

A road trip to south Georgia verified that, in fact, it was his vibrant vehicle to which she referred.

He phoned home to get some parental advice. "Yes ma'am. It looks great. It's full of animals, though."

"Alive or dead," said my mother.

"Stuffed animals. Bears."

"Go ahead and write a check for the fines. I'll buy the bears from you to defray the cost," she counseled. My brother, stunned, not because she advised him to acquire the van again, but because she wanted the multicolored carnival bears in its cargo, stammered, "Really?"

After hanging up, he approached the dried-up, pinch-lipped, humorless impound yard attendant. He desired to pay the minimum fine and free himself from further obligation, as well as drive the VW off the lot.

"But you're not the owner. You don't have a title. I can't release the vehicle to your custody."

Waving the letter from the state in the air, he replied, "The State of Georgia says I'm the owner."

"You sold the car," she retorted, in monotone.

"Okay then," said my little sib, "I don't want it and I won't pay for it."

She rolled her eyes at his idiocy. "The State of Georgia says you are the owner, and, therefore, you must either pay financial restitution or serve jail time for abandoning the vehicle."

Baby brother found himself in quite a conundrum, looking blankly at the woman, and thinking about the Grateful Dead and how many brain cells they may have inadvertently killed on their tours through Georgia.

He called dear old dad, who used connections to sort things out down in Auburn.

Driving home, my brother accidentally let one of the pink carnival bears whip out of the open window. At that moment he got a sick feeling in his gut. He suddenly discerned that our mother, a purveyor of ephemera, expected him to bring home taxidermied bears.

That Auburn jailhouse started to look pretty good.

As for me, I find none of this surprising, since nothing good ever comes out of a place named Auburn; especially when it comes to Georgia.

Hawg Killin'

During his tenure in law school at the University of Mississippi, my brother organized a hawg killin', and he spent a summer studying at Oxford in England; two things any well-bred southern boy ought to do somewhere along the line. Since I can sum up his England trip with bow-ties and tweed jackets, I'll reserve that story.

As for the hawg killin', however, as my brother tells it, he met some Yankee, communist students who desired to partake in the ritual of an all night pig roast, complete with PBR in the can. Under my sibling's tutelage, they bought vintage PBR with old-timey pop-tops from an eBay auction. Then they purchased a piglet from a Lafayette County farmer. They kept the beer in the fridge, and boarded the livestock in a dog pen, where they fed it cat food for ten months.

When the sow fattened, those communists dug a hole in their back-yard and fashioned an assembly of grill grates over the top. They admired their work, wondering how they would get that pig to lay still on those grates long enough for them to soak up the ambiance and drink the beer. Someone dumped a bag of cat food in the hole and lit it.

Knowing they needed help, they called reinforcements: A good ol' boy wannabe from Georgia, my brother. Thrilled about schooling Yan-kees in the proper handling of meat, he phoned our baby brother in Ath-ens. "You up for a hawg killin'," he asked. "These communists got a pig they need picked."

"Domestic or wild," inquired the younger one.

"Domestic."

"Not as much fun, but okay, I'm coming." So he packed up his .357 Magnum and left the communists in Athens to valiantly aid the ones in Oxford. He was more excited than 10 powerball winners from Alabama struggling to mathematically divide 73 billion dollars.

When the brother from Athens arrived, the law learnin' one pointed out the dog pen, and, thus, the target. A motley group of 9 communists, undone about kinks in their southern experience, stood around scratching the pig behind its ears and feeding it cat chow from their hands.

My brothers sauntered up like Wyatt and Virgil Earp and the circle of free-economy challenged men tightened around them, everyone eager to see just how a hawg killin' works.

"Never pull the trigger 'til it looks you in the eye," my baby brother whispered, so as not to startle dinner. The crowd leaning over the fence hushed and peered to see which way the porcine was looking.

BAM!

The communists jumped, ducked and wet their pants. A couple cried. The .357 Magnum dropped that pig like an American dropping a hot peso in Tijuana.

"We're fixin to show y'all how this is done," my brothers said to the group huddled behind the pen. The two men strung the hawg by its hind legs from the nearest tree, and bled it and gutted it, in short order. Then they dragged it to the pit, where the coals and cat food burned, and tossed it on the grates.

"Come on y'all," called my brothers, merrily ensconced in lawn chairs. "Get over here. All that's left is the sittin' and the eatin'."

But those communists now feared their pet, my brothers, and the .357 Magnum more than they feared capitalism. They chose to go out for a bite of humus, instead.

One brother said to the other, wistfully, "I believe the jury has spoken."

"Yeah," said the other, "a country boy can survive."

And they sat all night picking that pig, proud to be good Americans.

Just Making Conversation

Random dinner conversation rumbled on all sides of the table. Uncle Buck discussed the proper grilling technique for beef tongue. Cousin Hortel hitched, "Bless their hearts," to each commentary she undertook, in confidential whispers, on absent relations. And Grandmama Tyce tolerated her daughter-in-law, Ammaretta, screeching, "Can I gitcha somethin' to drink, Mama Tyce? Do you need me to take you to the potty, Mama Tyce? Let me wipe your mouth, Mama Tyce."

I don't know who said it, but, remarkably, the table silenced when a voice inquired, "Have y'all heard about the ban on fruitcakes in flight?"

I immediately thought of Ammaretta, until someone asked, incredulously, "People are using fruitcakes to take over planes?"

"You know," butted in Hortel, taking center stage, "we had a serious fruitcake incident in Botumsup, Alabama last Christmas. A case of domestic violence, sure enough. A woman didn't appreciate the hair curlers her husband put under the tree for her and cracked him over the head with his own mother's fruitcake. Near 'bout killed the man, bless his heart."

"I heard terrorists are planting explosives in them," offered another cousin. "Those red and green petrified cherries would penetrate flesh like holiday shrapnel."

"Cool," chimed in the children's tables.

"The Air Marshals would have to take me down before I'd give up a Bud McNeace fruitcake," my father-in-law challenged, rather heatedly.

"You still have one of those?" a surprised uncle asked. "How long has Bud been dead?"

"God bless him, he passed over eleven years ago, after a terribly long illness," my mother-in-law sighed.

The uncle started, "So, that would make the cake . . ."

"Nearly fourteen years old," finished my proud father-in-law.

"Eeeewwww," gasped the card table tykes.

This did not dissuade my husband's pa. With a gleam in his eye and fond memories of old Bud, he waxed forth about his holiday routine:

Each December, like an archeologist unearthing ancient artifacts, he digs the frosted fossil from where it sifted to the bottom of the freezer. When his fingers finally find the hunk enclosed in a Tupperwear container and wrapped in aluminum foil, his soul rejoices and joy abounds.

Gently he places the goody on the counter to thaw and pours himself a glass of brandy. (A spoonful of sugar they say . . .)

When the moment is right, he begins the unveiling, slipping the dessert first from its plastic tomb, and then carefully peeling away the aluminum mask. Beneath that lies the port stained cheesecloth cloaking the parcel remaining from the previous year.

He gazes lovingly at the beauty beneath the folds, knife poised to slice the annual sliver. Ceremoniously, the cut is made. The fork falls, and a decadent (his word, not mine) dollop, chased by a swig of brandy, satisfies his palate and sucks up his saliva (my words, not his). Finally, he takes time to ponder which heir he shall will it to, should he meet his demise prior to consuming the last crumb.

By the time my wistful father-in-law finished his account, we all sat, mouths agape; except for the children, who squawked a collective, "That's so gross."

An impressed Uncle Buck broke the awkward moment, asking, "How many years you think you got left in that baby?"

"Oh, I'd say about dozen, depending on how I carve it."

"If we don't have a fruitcake incident of our own, first," warned my mother-in-law.

Storing all this delectable data into her encyclopedia of family oddities and misfortunes, Cousin Hortel breathed, "Bless his heart."

I'm just glad my father-in-law doesn't have to travel by air to come for Christmas.

Jumping Through Hoops

My sister and her husband navigate through sweltering Alabama summers by pool hopping. On weekends, they lounge poolside at apartment complexes where friends live, once lived, or might live next year . . . or possibly in the next life.

Last Saturday found them alone next to shimmering blue water at Sussex Place West; "friends in residence" had taken a vacation or moved, or something.

Basking in the sun, my brother-in-law sweated profusely as his body temperature soared. He decided to take a dip. A child-size inner tube, featuring a 3D red Elmo with it's arms wrapped around the plastic top side, drifted in the otherwise undisturbed pool.

As he approached the edge of the deep end, near the abandoned floatie, my sister's spouse heard her, for a little fun, shout, "Betcha' can't dive through the tube."

"I can, but I'm not," he called back.

"I dare you," she taunted. Still, he refused.

"I double dog dare you." He shook his head, in response, with sweat pouring off his brow. Uncertainty prevails about whether the heat, or the anxiety over the dare, caused him to perspire like a fat lady at an all-you-can-eat raw vegetable buffet.

"I triple dog dare you!"

Well, there you have it. No man on earth can walk away from a triple dog dare with his masculinity intact. She verbally cornered her spouse, who had no choice but to capitulate.

Without saying anything, he turned, raised onto his toes, leapt into the air, and maneuvered his hulking torso toward the watery bull's eye. His hands deftly glided through the target, making way for his head and shoulders. Already, his brain screamed, "Hah! I told you so!"

Then it put out a Mayday call. The tube hit a little snag, as my sister's groom likes to put it. Feeling strong resistance and hearing a loud pop, in defeat he drifted noiselessly to the bottom of the pool, with Elmo hugging his midsection.

The fluttering tube made Elmo's hands wave helplessly at my sister, who stood on the pool deck wondering who she should call first, the paramedics or a good attorney.

At long last, her spouse surfaced, complaining of abdominal pain. They acted fast to remove the tube now cutting off the circulation to his head, feet and gut.

First they tried pulling it in the direction the momentum of the dive had started it. All that budged was my brother-in-law's liver. Next they attempted to heave Elmo back in the direction from which he arrived at this unpleasant location. Again, only flesh shifted and stretched.

Suddenly, as her beloved began to feel light headed from lack of oxygen, my sister had a brilliant idea. She lathered his belly with sunscreen. Then she pulled in one direction as the Greg Luganis impersonator backed away in the other. He shot out of his corset.

As he slid across the pavement on his bottom, he forgave his wife out of sheer relief. But they had no time to discuss the ordeal, because legitimate pool goers approached. Quickly, the pair reclaimed their positions in the chairs, leaving Elmo in a crumpled heap of plastic, slick with sweat and 30spf lotion.

A mama placed pool supplies on a table while her three year-old child scanned the water for his adored Elmo. The interlopers knew the child had discovered it when he let out an agonized yelp, dropped dramatically to his knees, cradled his flotation device and sobbed, "Oh Elmo, you are dead."

Meanwhile, the muppet mauler wrapped a towel around his blazing ring of fire and skulked away.

Weaving a Tangled Web

My brother's ex-wife offhandedly, and dangerously, remarked that I have yet to "victimize" her in my column. "Oh, but I have," I reminded her. "That stunt you pulled on your wedding day, having a wedding pawn read the scripture advising wives to submit to their husbands, that mind game made print, my dear."

"Oh, yeah, that," she smiled devilishly.

She is the quintessential southern belle, gracious to a fault, knows the importance of keeping up appearances, believes in nourishing the souls of others with comfort foods, and practices her womanly wiles so subtly only a lady of the same caliber could catch it. And she was smart to square off for the upper hand in her marriage at the outset, staging her rightful march to the matriarchal throne, right there at the nuptial altar; because she married my Mississippi brother, the space lawyer, who has said more than once, "The only way to cover up a lie is to tell a bigger one."

"Well, what have you done of note lately?" I inquired of her, interview style.

She thought for a moment, then offered, "I bought a tin of cinnamon roles at Bi-Lo, repackaged them, and gifted them to someone."

"Mm-hmm," I hummed, with a knowing, kindred nod. "Disguised them."

"Yes," she agreed. "But three days later his wife came asking for the recipe. I thought, 'Crap! Now he's dragged his wife into it. I don't have the recipe. Where's my lying husband when I need him? How will I get out of this gracefully?'

"How did you get out of it?" I grinned.

She leaned in and confided, "I told her it was a secret."

"True enough," I commended her.

Providing unnecessary self-defense, she continued, "I never told him they were homemade. He just assumed it because of the containers they were in, you know those disposable plastic containers you can buy at the grocery store. And then his wife assumed it was an old family recipe! I never said that."

"Who is he? Why did you take him cinnamon rolls, anyway?"

She sighed. "He's Mickey, the Program Manager of the Water Valley Main Street Association and I'm a member of the Water Valley Main Street Association Movie Night Committee. My job is to hang movie night posters around town. I ran out of time to do it, and I had to confess, and I had to give him the posters so someone else could put them up."

"So," I said, unraveling the tangled web, "you needed a sugar coated bribe to keep him from getting sideways with you. You led him to believe that you used the time, in which you could have hung the posters, slaving, instead, over the oven making homemade cinnamon rolls from a secret family recipe just for him."

Exhaling, she admitted, "I wanted the appearance of homemade without the trouble of it."

"Why didn't you just come clean?"

"I was so flattered that his wife wanted the recipe." Her hands flew in the air, as if she made a serendipitous discovery. "The flattery made me do it, made me tell this . . . this . . . tale." Then she gasped, "You're not going to put this in the paper are you? I hope my parents don't read it. Change my name to Caitlyn, better yet, Leye [our newest sister-in-law]," Kathryn said.

Regardless of what her parents think, my Mississippi brother will be pleased with how his ex-wife persisted in weaving that web into knots that'll never come out. That's because he doesn't know it's not lies as much as it's only mind games. Or, does he?

Follow That Baby

Even 9 months of erratic crying and unpredictable cravings did not prepare my husband for what lay beyond pregnancy. Fatherhood came abruptly to him, and by surprise, four times. It announced its arrival with phrases like, "I'm fine. Go get something to eat," then a change of heart, "Don't you dare leave this room," and a softening of heart, "Have you called your parents?" eventually topped off with, "I can't take you talking on the phone right now!"

My husband, dazed and confused, thinking, *My life will never be the same,* and fearing that I, having recently directed foul and venomous words at him, would come up out of the bed after him if he didn't obediently follow orders - "Don't lose sight of our baby" – chased after the nurse toting the highly prized bundle. His first official duty of fatherhood was to correctly identify, without a doubt, which one of those tiny, swollen-headed newborns belonged to us.

Remarkably, despite his abundant experience with the way babies come into the world, he never bothered to tell his own brother about what to expect at the culmination of pregnancy. He defensively explained his oversight to me, saying, "Unlike women, men don't have a compulsion to endlessly recount and compare birth stories."

In truth, though, as he stood by my brother-in-law peering through the wide nursery window, it occurred too late to my beloved that he omitted sharing critical highpoints of fatherhood. "Which one is yours?" my husband asked.

Rows of clear Plexiglas bassinets containing hours-old, sleeping babies faced the nurses on the other side of the room. The two men studied the swaddlings, immediately ruling out the pink ones. Finally, my brother-in-law pointed at the third bassinet from the right, proudly proclaiming, "That's him."

His wife's parents joined the men to gaze at their first grandchild. "He has your eyes," gushed the grandmother to the father. "His nose is from our side of the family," beamed the grandfather.

"He's a good looking kid for a newborn," expertly added the father of my children.

About that time, a nurse saw the four adults smiling and gesturing. My husband's brother motioned that he would like to check-out his child for a visit. She nodded, well acquainted with the eagerness of new parents.

Presently she wheeled the bassinet through the door into the viewing area. "Now don't get offended," she instructed the novice dad. "This is routine procedure. We do this with everyone. I need to check your bracelet against the baby's, Mr. Morris."

Stricken, my brother-in-law, Mr. Adams, looked at his in-laws and sibling, who all stared back, aghast, and in a small, tight voice said, "This isn't my baby."

The busy nurse didn't hear him and added insult to injury, grabbing his arm and checking his bracelet. "You're not Mr. Morris. This isn't your baby. I'll need to see if I can find your baby, Mr. Adams." She briskly retreated, taking Baby Morris with her.

A lump the size of Asia formed in my brother-in-law's throat. His wife's parents had witnessed his first unfortunate foray into fatherhood and would certainly make a report right away. My husband tried to help, saying, "If those babies weren't labeled, no one would know who they belong to. I mean, look at all those squished-up, red faces, and they're wrapped in blankets up to their cheeks and stocking caps pulled down to their eyebrows."

Then he started laughing, "But man, you broke the cardinal rule of fatherhood: Don't lose the baby."

Chapter Three

The Dog Years of Marriage

This afternoon, my husband, in one of those misguided moments of wanting to broaden the children's horizons and increase their scope of experiences and knowledge, gave the bandits an old computer to dismantle. In short order they disassembled it down to its bare gigabytes and sorted all the debris into colorful piles of pieces they plan to further break down into ever smaller and smaller megabytes and probably a whole lot of bits.

My husband didn't understand my irritation with him and his moment of indiscretion. He told me to take the microchip off my shoulder and let the children enjoy themselves. I guess it's been so long since he stepped barefooted on Legos in the dark, that his flash memory cannot recall the intense surprise and pain.

I can. And in the morning, without a doubt, as I stumble into the kids' rooms at 6am to wake them for school, some stray RAM will randomly access my tender heel by gouging its sharper edges deep into my flesh. Thinking about it makes this motherboard want to ROM away.

Anyway, one of the boys called me into his room a moment ago to show me a little gadget in his hand. It appears that dissection of technology has taken a strong hold on my offspring and opened up whole new micro-worlds to explore.

It also appears that my beloved will soon, as in forthwith, remember the pain and surprise of stepping on Legos in the dark, because my young lad got his disk drive so amped up about tearing into technology that he has taken apart all three of his father's remote controls.

New horizons, here we come.

Girls' Night Out

Girls' Night Out - PMS aside, it's the most dangerous night of the month for guys. It's the night husbands cook dinner (with every dish in the kitchen), bathe children (but don't hang up the towels), and read bedtime stories (Sports Illustrated, the swimsuit edition).

Meanwhile, we women dine and w[h]ine, (or do we w[h]ine and dine?). And we talk, and talk, and talk. And we whisper, followed by loud, table-slapping laughter, making all the males in the restaurant squirm uncomfortably in their seats; their paranoia leading them to believe that we have, with our teeth, verily skinned the dignity from one of their own.

I say paranoia because we really don't talk about men . . . much. We talk about shoes and purses, paint chips and fabric swatches, bra sizes and breast feeding, hairdressers and highlights, bathing suits and body fat, eyebrows and bikini waxes, plastic surgeons and the arts, garden club and gift wrap, and anyone who couldn't make it that night.

Regardless, our husbands all believe that we sit for hours absorbed in conversation about them. As if!

When I attend these therapy sessions, my one-and-only waits up. And thus, it's also the most dangerous night of the month for females.

"Who was there, tonight," he asks, pestering me until I list off names. "What did y'all talk about?"

"We discussed signing up for ballroom dancing and planning a girls' weekend at the Ritz and how fast our children's feet grow," I tell him.

"You did not," he protests, ignoring the ballroom dancing thing. "You talked about us," meaning himself and his fellow victims.

"Sort of."

He knew it. He just knew it.

"Someone suggested that we should advise our daughters to marry nerds. Nerds make the best husbands." I guardedly await his response.

"Who's married to a nerd? Which husbands fit that bill?"

I shake my head. "Only two or three men were mentioned by name." After a pause to consider how to proceed, I cautiously add, "You were not one of them." His face expresses relief at not getting labeled a Sherman, but it quickly clouds over, signaling that he can't decide if that's a good thing.

"Tell me who," he lobbies.

"Ahh, I cannot reveal identities," I reply, hoping to end the interrogation. "We each cut a palm with a butter knife. Then, pressing wounds together, we swore each other to secrecy. I cannot break the bond. It's treacherous enough that I'm sharing sacred information from the circle of trust with an outsider."

"Whatever." He glares at me, then lays a trap. "Did you tell them I'm a nerd?"

With no safe way to win this word game, I mutter, "Why would I?"

"You don't think I'm a good husband?"

"You're a great groom, but not exactly geeked-out on pocket protectors. Don't worry so much about what we say, anyway."

"I know how women are," he snaps.

"Okay," I confess, "sometimes we complain about y'all leaving your socks and shoes on the floor in front of the sofa. And we agree that we can read your minds when you come home from work, hug on us in the kitchen, and insist that we have a glass of wine. But mostly, we don't talk about y'all, at all."

Unconvinced, he queries, "Did you say anything about me tonight?"

"Yes. I told them what a superhero of a husband you are." [He glows.] "And that if you would start wearing your underwear on the outside of your pants everyone else would know it, too."

I laugh in the face of danger.

We Be Jammin': Island Living Country Style

My husband and I entered the dingy yellow building, walking beneath a dangling sign that read Fresh Seafood. Blown relentlessly by the salty wind coming off the marsh, it beat against the block building. We smiled at our escape to the island.

Inside, the hot humidity settled again and again behind each pass of an oscillating fan. Pungent fish odor permeated the place.

There, behind several bins of ice displaying sundry ocean novelties, stood the same young woman as usual, as if she hadn't changed spots since our last visit, peering over, helping customers.

Today, somehow, she looked different. Something had changed. She smiled. Her eyes didn't seem so tired.

"Hey," we greeted. "What's good?"

"These jumbos with heads on just come off the boat. Four ninety-five a pound." She paused for a moment, cocked her head to the right and said, "Life ain't nothin' but a riddle, you know."

"What do you mean," queried my spouse, adding, "We'll take 5 pounds of those jumbos. What about these scallops. Fresh?"

"Them come in a couple days ago. 'Bout the same time I met up with my bi-logicle daddy; the one what sired me. I been lookin' fer him for years."

"That right? Give me a half pound of scallops."

She passed the shrimp over to me and scooped crushed ice into another plastic bag. "They let him out o' prison to come to my brother's funeral. It was one of them happy-sad kinda days. I saw him and I just knew. Reckon the giveaway is the same three teeth we're both missin'."

She pulled her lips back, pointed at the dark gaps in her smile, and placed the tip of her wiggling tongue in each.

"Mmm," my husband hummed, affirming our hostess. "Fish bitin' in the creeks?"

"Some. Couple men caught a hammerhead back in here and dragged it out to the river earlier today. But I won't know 'bout the fishin' this time next week. My daddy, he's gettin' outta prison and I'm takin' time off."

We nodded and smiled at her in our on-the-island way. "Then give me five of those mullet so I can take my boys fishing," said my husband. "And how about the crabbing?"

"They ain't runnin' yet. Gotta wait a couple more weeks for that. I'm real proud o' my daddy for not runnin' when he come to the funeral. He could've. Lots o' reasons to."

My beloved admired the squid splayed on their frozen bed, dreaming of what he could pull out of the back river on a line baited with such oddities.

The girl continued, "After the funeral he come on back to Maw-maw's place for Kentucky Fried Chicken. Bunch o' folks there. Weirdest thing happened. I was standing with Maw-maw clear across the room from my daddy, and I said to Maw-maw, 'My daddy needs some tea.'"

Other customers shuffled in. "So I fixed him some tea and took it over. Do you know what he said?" She paused.

"What?"

"He said, 'Thanks darlin'. That's just what I needed.' Ain't that strange? Like we been connected all these years since he went missin'."

"Yep," said my husband.

"Yep," I echoed.

"Yep," said a hurried woman behind us, not yet in island mode. But it didn't deter our storyteller.

"Daddy and me, we been bound to be together again. We're a lot alike. We go for the same pieces of fried chicken. We put the same amount of gravy on our mashed potatoes. Maw-maw kept tellin' us, 'Ya'll quit that now. Yer freakin' me out.'"

"Wow," someone standing near the chilled octopus gasped.

"How much do we owe you," I inquired.

"Forty-two seventy-three."

We paid and wished her luck with her daddy getting out of prison and all. Back in the car, my husband slid Bob Marley into the CD player and remarked, "I love island living country style."

Superfecta

Natives of Louisville, Kentucky pronounce it loo-a-vul, or shorten it to luv-al, spoken from the top of the throat. Bluebloods say it through closed teeth, hardly moving their lips, and only a commoner would pronounce the s or, heaven forbid, say loo-ey. This is all the evidence anyone needs to know that Louisville is the northern-most southern city and not the southern-most northern city.

(Well, that, and Churchill Downs, and the Kentucky Derby, and Mint Juleps, and bourbon, and yes ma'am, and y'all.)

So, during a recent visit, I sought to straighten out exactly how to say Churchill. I asked our hosts, "Is it Church-hill, Church-ill, or Church-ul?"

Silence.

"It's not a dumb question," I defended myself.

"It's dumb," someone said.

Once we arrived at the track and found our box I sent my husband to get a program and Mint Juleps, which I discovered are not at all what the name implies. They are not minty. They are not sweet. They are not green. They do not have creamy froth on top.

Surprisingly, a Mint Julep tastes like straight brown liquor over ice with a sprig of fresh mint for garnish. And it wasn't long before I brought up the whole Church-hill, Church-ill, Church-ul debate.

"Here," my beloved said, handing me the program, "pick a winner for the next race."

"How can I tell which one will win?"

"That's the whole idea behind gambling," he said, taking away my drink.

Off we waltzed to the Paddock, determined to gamble away the children's college tuition $2 at a time. As the jockeys and horses paraded by, I started selecting possible winners.

"Ooh, number thirteen. Look how handsome he is. Short, but handsome."

"Lucy, you can't pick a horse based on how the jockey looks."

"Why not?"

"Because number thirteen has only placed in two of its last fourteen races," he said, directing me to the stats in the program. Then to bolster his logic with reason he added, "And thirteen isn't a lucky number."

Thirteen won. But we bet on 10.

Next race, I announced, "Put it all on Grease Monkey. I like the name."

I readied a big I-told-you-so as Grease Monkey slipped around the track a full body length ahead . . . until the final one hundred yards. He finished last . . . by a full body length.

A new strategy developed. "Number four," I said. "He has pink and green silks. It's like a Lilly Pulitzer fashion show."

"Then let Lilly pick four. The odds are twenty to one. Let's go with number seven. The jockey has black and white checked silks like a NAS-CAR flag. I bet that horse is fast."

It wasn't.

Still, some folks were winning big money at the track. The superfecta paid out $1200 in one race, $34,000 in another, and $68,000 in yet another. The numbers provided inspiration. My husband disappeared and came back with another Mint Julep, for me, and a bet stub for himself. The superfecta - horses 7, 3, 1, and 11, in that order.

Eleven bolted out of the gate followed by 1 and 3. Seven worked to close the gap. As the field of horses entered the last turn my soulmate exuberantly yelled about Daddy buying dinner tonight and baby getting a new pair of shoes.

They crossed the finish line in correct order. He steadied himself and grabbed my Mint Julep and took a long swig. We pensively waited for payouts to flash on the board in the infield.

Clarfication of the pronunciation of Churchill flashed up in bright lights –

Superfecta payout: $17.50.

Church-uuhhhhhlph.

Commode Diving

Last night, more than fifteen years of marriage came to a head. I wasn't five minutes behind my husband going upstairs, but by the time I got there he was ensconced in the bed, under the covers, with all the lights off. Ignoring his harrumphing and pillow slapping, I clicked on the switch and headed to the bathroom, using the ambient glow from the bedroom to put on my pajamas and brush my teeth.

No Tom Bodett, my one-and-only didn't leave the light on for me. As I turned from the sink toward the door, sudden darkness fell. My right foot stepped awkwardly on an unseen shoe. Before I could swing my left foot forward and plant it firmly on the tile floor, my torso wheeled and wobbled, pitching me sideways. My left foot lifted higher and higher as I struggled through the strange reflexive contortions of my upper body, and my arms waved in opposing circular motions, reaching blindly for stability and balance.

In the midst of this emergency, my brain quipped, *I'm going to kill whoever left that shoe in the floor*, but didn't dwell on it long because downward descent had begun, and I immediately knew on whom to blame my predicament. And he was in the bed calling, "Lucy? Lucy? Are you okay?"

No time to answer. My hands went from scraping the air to breaking my fall. Grabbing and grappling, I sent the iron toilet paper stand crashing beneath me, prompting my man to check again, from between the sheets, "What's happening?"

The fingers on my left hand finally grasped the wicker side table. My right hand, however, still plunged into empty space, precipitously sliding down something wet and cold, fingers working to take hold of safety but only massaging a smooth, slick surface. A hard edge caught my elbow. Gravity yanked me down onto the trash can as my hand scrambled in the dark for a grip, until it touched water.

Five seconds after my beloved cussed and turned off the bedroom light, I lay limply on my back, a wrought iron pole poking my spine, trash scattered, my hip resting on the battered waste basket, and my arm dangling in the toilet.

And my husband bravely yelling, from the bed, "Are you hurt? Answer me!"

Hurt?! I'd been telling that man for fifteen plus years to close the toilet lid when he flushes. And there I was, sprawled on the bathroom floor like an old lady with a broken hip (which I hadn't yet ruled out), thinking I was going to have to tuck some dirty underwear under my head for a pillow, and wait for the children to find me in the morning.

Regaining my wits, I furiously removed my dripping fingertips from the commode, dragged myself to the sink, weakly pulled up, and scrubbed like a surgeon. Still the man demanded a report. "Could you just shut up?" I barked.

I crept to the bathroom light switch. I wanted evidence of guilt. But, seeing the criminal tennis shoe, I started to cry. It was mine. Then, struck by the irony, I got so tickled, I couldn't catch my breath.

My groom started again, from the bed, "Are you okay?"

I'd been to the bottom of the toilet bowl and back, but I wasn't broken, and I didn't have to spend the night with his smelly drawers shoved under my cheek; yes, I was okay.

I climbed under the covers, forgiveness in my heart, and reached out to snuggle him. "Which arm was it?" he asked.

An evil giggle slipped out.

This morning, after more than fifteen years, he closed the toilet lid.

Pura Vida

Perched in the open-air, Costa Rican airport, awaiting our flight back to cold reality, I commented to my husband, "Perhaps I'll make it to spring now."

"Perhaps," he mumbled, thinking, *Perhaps, perhaps not,* the warm breeze sifting through his hair.

Four hours later, stewardesses opened the plane portals and waved adios. Customs was a Babylon of nationalities and languages, all driven like livestock into chutes. Customs officers woofed random orders – Move forward, stand back, shift left, step right, Simon didn't say, sit down.

Or what? I sarcastically breathed. *Get sent back to paradise?*

Barkers corralled off U.S. citizens from the less fortunate. As we shuffled into an extraordinarily long line, a man cut in front of me. He didn't even blanch under my hairy-eyeball glare. I hoped the weasel would get detained in Customs, for hours.

All the same, my husband and I eventually stepped across the formidable, yet glorious, yellow stripe that marks the boundary between limbo and U.S. soil. We approached the window and presented our passports.

The officer looked at my passport, at me, at his computer screen, typed, gazed at my passport, me, and passed back the document. Then he picked up my husband's papers. He checked the passport, studied my husband, typed, checked, passport, husband, passport, husband, computer screen, passport – until I knew I would squirm right out of my shoes and make a full confession of something any minute. Still holding my husband's proof of citizenship, the officer gruffly commanded, "Come with me."

Line-Cutter smirked when he saw us escorted away. My inner voice quipped, *And a gloater, too. I wonder if his mama knows.*

In the holding room, I whispered, "What have you done?" But I felt strangely culpable. *Is it the coffee? The seashells? A case of a guilty conscience worn on a sleeve?* Another Customs officer interrogated my beloved about everything from his mother's name to details of the last time he picked fuzz from between his toes.

The man took my passport. *Oh my gosh! They think I'm an accomplice to an international fugitive!* Fear of a future behind bars gripped my heart.

As I began composing my speech about innocence and mercy and being a teacher and mother, it struck me: *Oh my gosh! They think I'm an accomplice to an international fugitive!* The thrill erased all my fear. I envisioned the airport atwitter with travelers discussing how they witnessed us, the Sunbathed Bandits, getting hauled off to the backrooms and bowels of the airport, detained in Customs. Our intrigue and mystique multiplied a hundred fold in that one instant.

I imagined our lonely luggage revolving on the baggage carousel and tourists standing around speculating about its contents and when security would come blow it up. I pictured them nodding, saying how normal and mild-mannered we seemed and mentioning how our delicious drawls made words slide off our tongues like pats of melting butter. Con artists or spies, they all conclude, wandering off to their ordinary, humdrum lives, shaking their heads, agreeing that you never can tell about people.

A grouchy, "Why would they issue me a passport? If I'm on the Most Wanted List?" briefly interrupted my fantasy.

"They were hoping you would leave and never come back to menace America again," I explained to him with dramatic flair. I informed him of our Bonnie and Clyde fame circuiting over cell phones in nearby corridors.

He harumphed. I reminded him, "We're still on vacation until we pull into our driveway." We waited for our hosts to sort out the case of mistaken identity. I said, "Perhaps, now, we'll make it to spring."

"Perhaps," he replied. I knew what he was thinking, though.

98 Dog Years

My friend, Charlotte, and her husband celebrated their 10th wedding anniversary on December 28th. Charlotte, always sensible, says that any couple who makes it to the ten year mark can make it to eternity; or at the very least, through the dog years of marriage. She's looking forward to them.

Her husband, always sentimental, to commemorate the momentous event, went in search of the perfect gift, a traditional present. Being a man, he obviously visited a jewelry store, thinking it must have anything a woman would want from the opposite sex.

When he explained to the young lady behind the sparkling glass case how he wished to shower his wife with a customary gift of aluminum and tin for their 10th anniversary, she looked sympathetically at him, and then his wallet. Shaking her head compassionately, she directed him to the nearest hardware store.

When he turned to leave, a seasoned sales lady, seeing her protégé allow a man primed to have his pocket picked simply sashay out the door, clutched his elbow.

"What is it again that you're looking for darling?" she asked, redirecting him back to the center of the sales floor. Smartly dressed and tastefully accessorized, the older woman spoke with an all-knowing sophistication.

"A gift for my wife to mark surviving a decade of marriage," he repeated.

"Oh, well, you're looking for diamonds, then" she purred. "We have a vast selection of the loveliest diamonds in a variety of settings for rings, bracelets, necklaces, earrings, and tiaras. I know we can find just the right remembrance to impress your bride."

She would have continued her sales spiel except that he interrupted her to say, "Uh, not diamonds. The list on the Internet said aluminum and tin."

Curling her lip disdainfully, peeved at the Internet for allowing commoners access to information, she snorted, "Oh, you saw the other list." She enunciated other with disgust as thick as sorghum syrup. "No one uses that list anymore. It's so outdated."

Her customer's eyes bulged as she tightened the noose around his neck, and her grip around his upper arm, in an attempt to cut off the oxygen to his brain. Carefully, the clerk slipped on her reading glasses, sliding them to the point of her nose so she could stare down her challenger over the top rim. Then she unfolded the new list and, like a magician with a slight of hand, showed him *Tenth Anniversary – Diamonds*.

Hastily, she re-folded the paper and slipped it back into her pocket. Charlotte's husband, a quick witted man, whose suspicions got the best of him, cast a furtive glance at the new list before she put it away. He wouldn't swear to it, but he thinks he saw the recommended presents for the 1st, 7th, 16th, and 45th anniversaries – all diamonds.

My theory on this is simple: Jewelry stores have it tough these days. Few marriages make it to the typical diamond anniversary. So, to boost sales, jewelers banded together and reworked the list, in dog years.

Anyway, looking for an exit strategy, and backing toward the door, Charlotte's groom said, "I thought diamonds were forever. I haven't been married forever, yet, only ten years."

On January 16th, my husband and I will celebrate our wedding anniversary. The old list says we should exchange mementos of ivory; traditional, but not politically correct. I don't expect I'll get a carved elephant tusk or the like.

Don't fret, dear. The 14th anniversary is actually the 98th in dog years, and since that's practically forever by today's standards, I'll settle for the diamonds.

The Sordid Affairs of Chicken Nuggets

I shook my tumbler and clinked the ice to alert my partner that the bottom of my glass was more arid than the Sahara. He glanced in my direction, annoyed that I would snap my fingers for him to serve me in front his male counterparts.

Of course, I will claim now that he misinterpreted my intentions. I never meant to belittle him in front of the guys or make him look like he waits on me hand and foot. I just wanted him to be a gentleman. Besides, he was closest to the bar. We have a general rule in our relationship: whoever is closest to whatever the task is has to do it. That obligation is only escapable if the one says to the other, "Let's do it together."

But that's not what he said. He cocked himself back in his chair, puffed out his chest, crossed his arms and asked, "What will you give me?"

Not having my purse with me, I had to think quickly. My mind raced around until it leapt into the backseat of my car. I blurted out, "A chicken nugget!" because that's mostly what I've got in my car, other than little boys' smelly socks.

A low, "Ooooooh," laced with an, "Uhhhhh, huhhhhhh," gurgled at the back of throats, boiled out of the mouths of the men and women sharing our table.

One of my husband's buddies chided, "You better get that lady a drink, cause you gonna get some chicken nuggets tonight." He dragged out "chicken nuggets" in a sordid manner, that only a man can.

My face turned bright red.

A girlfriend sitting to my left lifted her glass off the table, pushing it toward her spouse, and declared, "See about getting me a refill, baby. I'll give you two chicken nuggets."

Since she has as many children as I do, I knew she could follow through with the deal. All the fellas half stood and high-fived each other across the table.

The whole time this scene played out, I stammered, "Ya'll don't understand. I'm talking about chicken nuggets," which was answered by an anonymous male voice saying, "Mmmm, hmmm. That's what I'm talkin' 'bout too." Everybody laughed.

Then the analysis of the dear chicken nugget began. "A nugget might be alright. But it's such a little morsel. It takes so many to fill me up," said one guy, who promptly swiped his wife's half-empty glass and sprinted to the bar like a hungry fellow trying to earn as many nuggets as he could handle in one night.

"Yeah," said another. "And those nuggets are just parts is parts. You never know what you might get. I think I'd rather have the whole breast."

"Heck, honey," a third added, giving his wife a special wink, "I think I'll take the whole chicken."

This time the guys fist pumped each other while the chickens all rolled their eyes.

Finally, one of the women responded. "No man has ever cared what part he got so long as he got it. You wouldn't even know how to handle the whole chicken. I've a mind to say no nuggets for you."

At this remark, the men at the table laughed even louder and pointed out to their friend how he had been dissed.

Together, all the females at our table repeated, "No nuggets for any of you."

The lady across the table from me pointed at her significant other and assured him, "The only chicken nuggets you'll be getting tonight are from Micky D's."

Seeing themselves now on the losing side of this battle to berate the chicken nugget into an unmentionable, which it normally is in the adult world anyway, the men started hopping to take care of their dates, and ultimately, themselves. Drink glasses never drained again that night.

And I thought to myself, Micky D better not give my one and only any chicken nuggets. I've got plenty for him on the backseat of my car. That's where he likes to get his and that's where I keep the really nasty ones.

And you, my friend, better pull your head up out of the gutter; because you know as well as I do what I'm talking about.

Don't Doubt Me

Midway through our evening family meal, the phone rang. I stood up to lift the receiver from the hook, but it cut short of finishing its one and only bbbbbrrrrrrring. Unable to stop my reach-and-grab reflex as quickly as the caller dissed me, I held an empty receiver in my fist. Looking at it, feeling a sudden sense of rejection, I sighed, "Hmmm."

Then I returned to my seat and said, earnestly, to the people who love me most in this world, "Wow. That was life changing. Think how different things could have been if the phone hadn't rung. My fate may have taken off in a completely different direction."

Being minors and having no choice, my children accept my frequent but brief philosophical outbursts. But my husband objected, "You can't be serious." Nodding toward our eating offspring, he asked, "Why are you filling their heads with this nonsense?"

"I am serious," I persisted. "I can't tell you what's different or what would have been, but that was a pivotal moment. Probably, all moments are, but that one was punctuated with sound."

"You treat me so wrong," he accused.

"You love me for it," I said, before I called him out. "Why do you doubt my sincerity? That's the second time you've doubted me today."

"It is? What did I doubt you about first?"

"You didn't believe I meant it when I told you to put your red lift on display when you retire it," I reminded him.

"It's a dumb idea," he countered.

My husband is the original owner of the only red Nifty Lift ever imported to America. He special ordered it painted Georgia Bulldog red. I hit on the idea of making the lift a tourist attraction when I suggested that he send a picture of himself operating it to the UGA athletic department so they could see how he expresses his Georgia pride.

Then, the juices in my gray matter started percolating and one thought led to another until I had the machine on a pedestal in front of my beloved's store, the county's tourism department listing it in travel brochures, and the state posting brown signs on the interstate announcing the place of interest and the exit number. I even visualized tourists standing in line for bucket rides and photo-ops.

"Why do you goad me this way," he complained.

"I'm not joking. I'm on to something. I'm a marketing genius. Your lift would become a town landmark. People would say, 'Go down yonder 'bout a mile past the red Nifty Lift at the rental store and turn left. You cain't miss it. It's the only red one ever imported to America.'"

"I'm starting to think . . ."

I cut him off, "Well, stop."

"No, I'm starting to think . . ." he tried again.

"You should stop now," I advised.

Frustrated, he griped, "What are you talking about?"

"If you're just now starting to think after all these years, why bother? It could get you into trouble. Just leave thinking to me. I've got your back."

"I'm starting to think," he irritatedly repeated, "that you say all these crazy things to drive me over the brink so you can collect the insurance money."

Our amused, chewing children, who witnessed this volley from start to abrupt end, giggled like seventh grade girls in the school bathroom.

I say these things because I firmly believe God put us here to amuse each other and bring happiness to the world, starting at home with the people we love and going from there.

(But I'm serious about the lift.)

Snapping over Snapple

Change requires work; therefore, I resist it, ignore it, put my hands over my ears singing, "Lah, lah, lah, lah," and otherwise stagnate in stability.

My husband, a crawdad of a different color, bores easily. If the road shows signs of travel, he finds a new route; no matter that he loses his direction. He courts adventure.

Regardless of our differences, we have in common the fact that we can't drive around the block without stopping at a convenience store for a bottled beverage. And, as it's my spouse's chivalrous duty to go in and purchase our drinks, I always request a Snapple, by name. "If they don't have Snapple," I add, "get me something like it."

To my consistent disappointment, he never fulfills my one request. He exits every store, tail tucked between legs, offering me all types, flavors, brands, and makes of drinks, but never a Snapple – or anything like it.

Finally, after weeks, months, nay, years, of holding my tongue, last Wednesday, I asked him, "Why don't you ever buy me a Snapple?"

"Why do you always want a Snapple," he asked, quite indignantly, as if I was the one at fault.

"It doesn't necessarily have to be a Snapple," I snapped. "As I have said before, any equivalent would do."

He breathed deeply and glared. Then pointing at the strawberry-kiwi-mango mixture I held, he exasperatedly challenged, "Drink up. That's as close as I can get. What do you expect, anyway?"

"Iced tea," I sharply retorted. "Snapple means iced tea."

Sighing heavily, he went on to explain that Snapple does not mean, and has never meant, iced tea. First of all, according to my knowledgeable and worldly spouse, tea is only iced if it has ice in it and beverage bottlers don't put ice in tea. Secondly, Snapple's main product line consists of fruity drinks. "Iced tea is a hobby," he declared, "a sideline to garner extra revenues. If Snapple means anything, it means fruit drink."

After that he dropped the mothball bomb, cutting me to the quick.

"Besides," he taunted, "I never see Snapple in stores anymore. I think the company went out of business. In 2010, ordering a Snapple is like when you say you need to AVAIL cash, or that you want to watch a video tonight. And why do you keep writing tin foil on the grocery list? Modern man uses aluminum foil, grandma."

Momentarily I sat in silence picking at the label on the fruity knock-off beverage in my hand, my bottom lip poking out. "I have the right to rent a beta-max movie without you tossing out slurs on prehistory," I sassed.

He ignored my comment and continued, saying, "If you want iced tea just say iced tea. I get stressed out every time I go in a store looking for Snapple. I never bring out the right thing and you always look irritated. Snapple means fruit drink. Fruit drink, fruit drink, fruit drink!"

We lapped the block in silence, sipping to ourselves. I made a mental note of his transgression against me, icebox owners, and Snapple lovers everywhere.

When we got home, I logged onto the Internet, plugged in Snapple. com, crossed my fingers, closed my eyes, said a prayer, and clicked. The search engine churned.

Then, as big as a cold pitcher of iced tea on an August afternoon, the Snapple home page popped onto my screen. And the headliner product was (drum roll please) . . .

SNAPPLE TEA. SNAPPLE TEA. SNAPPLE TEA.

Hah! I win!

(A lesser Cro-Magnon woman than me would gloat for another ten thousand years.)

Romance is in the Ritz of the Beholder

Charlotte's boys and my boys went to camp for a full week, leaving us with only our girls (and our husbands). So Charlotte and I cooked up a little plan for romance. I would keep her girls two days and nights so she and her husband could get some alone time, and she would do the same for me.

We thought ourselves ingenious.

Charlotte's husband went right to work arranging a get-away. While we sat by the pool, Charlotte checked her cell messages. A big grin spread across her face.

"What?" I questioned her.

"Listen to this," she bragged, handing me the phone. Her husband's voice invited, *Char, meet me at the Ritz. I'll be there by 5:15. Look for the bald guy at the bar drinking a scotch and water.*

My husband had his own romantic plan. "We're going to get your list checked off."

"Rewind the tape. I didn't hear that right."

"You wrote 30 things on your summer to-do list. If we don't get some of it done, you'll be a weed in my garden by the end of summer," he accused.

My beloved says I have ADD, that I only get partial projects done because I get distracted by the next shiny thing I see. As proof of this he cites the time his friend Campbel saw me in the front yard and dropped by to say hello. According to my husband, Campbel reported that I was pulling weeds.

"What's ADD about that?" I asked my spouse.

"You had your purse over your shoulder."

Needless to say, we worked on my list.

On the first day together, sans children, we painted the porch furniture. While we had rocking chairs dragged out in our front yard, Charlotte arrived to get my daughter's bathing suit. Charlotte rambled on about taking the kids to the pool for a cool dip; all the while I sweated and labored, sanding, priming, and painting tables and chairs.

Surveying the scene, Charlotte remarked, mockingly, "This definitely doesn't look like the Ritz."

I wanted to tell her she wasn't being very ladylike, but I couldn't bring myself to talk that way in front of our daughters, who tagged along behind her.

That night my one and only took me to dinner at a dingy, cement floored, graffitied, seat-yourself restaurant. He had coupons.

We went on a date because he had coupons.

The next day we hung blinds in the sunroom and pictures on the walls. At least we weren't in the blazing sun.

That night he took me to a movie with a lot of foul language and shocking scenes. Then we went to get a bite to eat. This time he did not choose the place based on a discount. And a hostess seated us. Still not the Ritz, but improving.

When our food and beverages arrived, my soulmate gallantly extended an unfolded napkin toward me. He placed his gum in it and nodded for me to do the same. Then he gingerly refolded the paper into a wad and placed it to the side; our masticated chewing gum set together for eternity.

I pictured an archeologist finding the entwined pieces two thousand years hence and drawing conclusions about the mating rituals of technologically primitive people.

A girl has to find romance where she can.

When we got home, I crossed three things off my summer to-do list. It felt great, sort of like how I imagine a night at the Ritz might. Next summer, maybe my husband will be brave enough to let me find out if I'm right.

Chapter Four

Chain of Fools

The first day back from our holiday break, one of my Pre-K students ran to the carpet for circle time. But not before impulsively grabbing, touching, breaking, and pushing as many toys and people as possible along the way; typical tornado-like behavior for this particular child, much to the annoyance of classmates. Sitting down, he excitedly blurted, with a genuine smile, "I missed my friends so much."

The boy next to him, a gentle little lad who seldom said a harsh word to anyone, looked the other boy directly in the eye, and challenged, "What friends?"

Chicken Ranch Chronicles

T he on-line ad read, *Those pastel, peeping presents left by the Easter Bunny have inspired you. You want to start a chicken ranch. Don't let the nay-sayers get you down. With this step-by-step instructional DVD, anyone, even you, can farm roosters and hens. Send $14.95 plus $17.50 for S&H to Fowler Ranches Nvrben, 800 Scratchnpeck Butte, Hiroost, CA 85409.*

When I discovered that she showed my children a chicken ranch video made in California, the hair on the back of my neck stood up. It aroused images of a seedy documentary about a Nevada house of ill-repute.

I also wondered, living in a rural county like we do, laden with farmers and FFA boys willing to jaw about raising chickens until the cows come home, why Charlotte bypassed the experts and clicked **Add to My Shopping Cart.**

Four to six weeks later the DVD arrived via U.S. postal service. Charlotte dropped it on top of the television, forgetting about it until Saturday, when my four children went over to play with her four children.

By mid-afternoon, Charlotte wanted to stick a hot poker up her left nostril and slowly twist it. "Hey, kids," she called, in a tremulous voice, as they howled through the house slamming doors, "how about a movie?"

Every child came running, except the one tethered to a chair. He hobbled in ten minutes later, raking his theater seating across the wainscoting in the hall.

Charlotte tapped **PLAY**, and wandered away to put a cold cloth on her forehead. Meanwhile, the babes in her care learned about conception.

"That rooster is pulling that hen's feathers out of her back," exclaimed one child.

"He's so mad at her," observed another.

"Now he's trying to squish her down. He's so mean.," said one of the girls.

Finally, a worldly brother, having logged more Animal Planet hours than Jeff Corwin, exasperatedly instructed, "They're mating, y'all."

"What's that," inquired a younger child.

"It's when one animal climbs on another one's back. Duh!"

Through time lapse, chickens hatched and developed from babies to adolescents to adults.

Just as the tykes started to fidget, the feature climaxed. The narrator talked, as a woman held a fat, brown hen by its ankles, wings flapping furiously and then helplessly hanging toward the earth.

The woman placed the chicken's neck between two rusty nails pounded into an old stump and, without warning, slung a hatchet blade down with the other hand. THWACK! A flick of the hand-ax scraped the head, beak opening and closing in a voiceless mercy plea, to the ground.

Eight children sucked in hard, their eyes drinking in the rivulets of blood running down the stump onto the dirt, while the voiceover droned on. Yet, no one looked away.

The hand, that moments before held the bloody hatchet, lifted the twitching body from the makeshift guillotine and placed it on the ground. Of course, to the glee and awe of the viewers, it ran.

THWACK! A second headless hen lay upon the stump. This time the woman lowered the body, neck down, into a bleed-cone (a milk jug recycled as a funnel), feet dangling over the sides. Gravity pulled the juice of life through the plastic spout.

Compared to the next sequence, boiling and plucking the flaccid corpse, the scalded rabbit scene from Fatal Attraction would have given our offspring warm fuzzies. And it wasn't until this carefully crafted videography that the children fled the room, screaming for Charlotte.

The upside to mentally scarring impressionable youths: They will probably never go within one hundred miles of a Nevada chicken ranch.

Mrs. Smith Goes to Washington

No doubt, the gentleman wondered what Mrs. Smith was doing in the private, men's lavatory in the White House China Room. No doubt, her unexpected intrusion made him very, very uncomfortable. No doubt, he suspected espionage, terrorism, or, worse, that she wanted to use the stall he currently occupied.

Mrs. Smith had good reason for being there – her daughter, Julia, made a wish. Julia has a rare and life-threatening blood disorder known as Glanzmann's Thrombasthenia. The Make-A-Wish Foundation contacted Julia's mother about granting Julia her heart's desire.

Mrs. Smith balked. First, she has not, does not, will not ever label Julia's illness terminal. In fact, she is certain a cure is imminent, and she, her one determined self, started the Glanzmann's Research Foundation to raise money to fund Dr. David Wilcox, a scientist seeking the cure.

Secondly, she didn't want to suffer Disney World, a common craving among Make-A-Wish kids. Like me, Mrs. Smith would rather eat a container of crickets than spend ten minutes in Mickey Mouse's mayhem.

Julia surprised her mother. She requested to meet the President. She had some burning questions for him, such as *Can you make yourself a sandwich in the middle of the night, or does someone else make it?* and *Do Barney and Miss Beazely sleep in the bed with you and Mrs. Bush?* and *Do you get to preview movies before anyone else?*

Thus, the Make-A-Wish foundation arranged a September 19th VIP visit with the leader of the free world.

That's how Mrs. Smith's family ended up in the White House Diplomatic Room with a butler serving them water from a silver tray. That's how Mrs. Smith nervously sipped several glasses, while awaiting the President's arrival. That's why their liaison conducted Mrs. Smith to the China Room gentlemen's facilities.

Mrs. Smith primped in the mirror (no self-respecting southern woman would dare meet the President without her face on straight) thinking how odd that a place so grand and beautiful would have stinky, old plumbing.

As she turned to push the stall open, and it didn't budge, she realized the nature of the situation. Accidentally, she spied, through the crack in the door, a man in the sitting position staring back at her. He never said a word in response to Mrs. Smith's profuse apologies she heaped upon him while skirting out to the safety of the Diplomatic Room.

At long last, in walked President George W. He rubbed his hands together in excitement and hop-stepped straight to Julia. "I've been looking forward to meeting you," he warmly said, accompanying that with greetings for each of her family members. Mrs. Smith received a kiss on the cheek.

Mr. President, after turning and accepting an item from his personal aid, presented Julia with a handsome, silver bookmark engraved with the presidential seal. Unfortunately, Mrs. Smith had difficulty focusing on the exchange, because she felt strangely familiar with the President's assistant and got distracted trying to place his face . . .

. . . which took her right back to the China Room latrine. The President's personal aid is a boxer man!

No doubt, he couldn't believe his bum luck. No doubt, he wished Mrs. Smith had been a threat to national security. No doubt, when recognition flitted between them, he wished he were lying in state in the rotunda.

For you inquisitive ones, yes, the President can make his own sandwich for a midnight nibble. Yes, Barney and Miss Beazely sleep in the bed with them, but also have their own west wing room. Yes, he gets to preview movies while snacking on his favorite snack – popcorn.

(To find out more about the Glanzmann's Research Foundation and the Make-A-Wish Foundation, visit www.CureGT.com and www.wish.org, respectively.)

The Do's and Don'ts of Kitten Reallocation

Last week a fellow teacher sent around an e-mail: Does anyone know of someone who would like to have a kitten?

I replied: *Yes, 188 elementary school students.*

Coincidentally, Charlotte called the next day asking if I knew anyone who needed a kitten, to which I quipped, "No one ever needs a kitten."

This hullabaloo over infant felines got me pondering the proper protocol for disposing of them. The sack and rock method no longer in fashion, what should one do, say, when she arrives home, four children piling out of the minivan with her, to find a defenseless kitten under an oak tree on the line between her house and her neighbor's?

Although experience is the best teacher, sometimes we learn just as well from Charlotte's mistakes. So, for the benefit of readers, with Charlotte's assistance for illustrative purposes, I present the unequivocal list of Do's and Don'ts of kitten reallocation.

DON'T let your children see the kitten. Remain vigilantly alert for unusual movement or squeaky mewing in the foliage. Unfortunately, just as Charlotte's did, your youngsters will likely detect the kitten before you.

DON'T let your kids touch the kitten. Yell, as they sprint toward it, "Do not pick up that animal! It has germs and it will bite you or scratch you and make you sick!" As they gallop on without regard, shout, "I'm gonna spank every one of you if you pick up that nasty kitten!" Of course, just like Charlotte's brood, they'll probably pick it up anyway.

DON'T take it to the neighbor's house, even though it was partially on her property line, knock on her door, and say, "Hi, Miss Sarah. We found your kitten. I brought it back so you can feed it. It's crying like it's hungry." Not only will she politely, but swiftly, close the door in your face, but you also can't sneak and leave the bundle on her doorstep.

DON'T let your children see you taking it to the neighbor's house. They will cry pitifully. Plus, if you stealthily deposit the creature at her door, they'll let it slip later that you were the one who left it there.

DON'T call your friend down the street, (in Charlotte's case, that would be me), and leave a voicemail message that says, "Hey! Hope you're having a great day! I found your black kitten at my house. Call me when you get home and I'll bring it down." (Yeah, right.)

DON'T take the kitten to the vet [Charlotte]. The doctor will observe its paws, pull its skin, inspect its gums, and put his stethoscope to its belly.

Then he'll solemnly shake his head, making you feel even more obligated to provide care, prescribe an antibiotic and vitamins that you must administer through a dropper three times a day, and hand you a bill so big you question after the kitten's certain pedigreed breeding.

DO leave it at the home of children, preferably ages 10 and under.

DO place it under a shady tree, close enough to the house so it will be found, but far enough away that it looks like it wandered up.

DO drop it off when no one is home.

DO as Charlotte resourcefully did and manipulate your kids into leaving the kitten at the Humane Society in exchange for purchasing two fish from the pet store; quickly close the deal and complete the transaction.

OR, take a streamlined track, and **DO** what I suspect my coworker did - Put the kitten under the oak tree on the line between Charlotte's house and the neighbor's.

To Kill a Magnolia Tree

She's gone and done it now. Charlotte, ignoring all my warnings, all her home training, cut down a magnolia tree. Such an act, for any reason, sits on par with the sins of disparaging Elvis, forgetting your yes ma'ams, spelling y'all incorrectly, asking a lady her age, and killing mocking-birds.

When I said, "You dare not cut down that huge magnolia. Especially when it's still in full, fragrant bloom," Charlotte put her hands over her ears and sang, "La, la, la, la, I can't hear you," and felled it anyway.

Her daddy, chagrined, assured her there's a law against cutting down magnolias. "That's live oaks, Daddy," Charlotte corrected.

"Baby girl, you think you know so much. But I'm telling you, around here the law deals with magnolias." Having served as sheriff of this county for 30 years, he probably knows.

Charlotte's mama, bless her heart, could only shake her head, shamed at her daughter making a spectacle of the family like that. After all, they have to suffer the stain of her indiscretion on their good name.

"I think cutting down a magnolia is bad luck," I advised her, trying to go a little easier on Charlotte than her kinfolks. "It's a crime against nature, like denigrating the iron cross, spitting on the sidewalk, forgetting to apply lipstick, or building a house without a porch. Mark my words, something bad will happen. Your eyebrows might get bushy and grow together."

Noting her disregard for my reproach and consumed by worry for the salvation of her southern soul, I shared the story of my baby brother, hoping it would help her see the error of her ways and inspire her to set things right.

My baby brother grew up in the shadow of a family crest emblazoned with the words, *Everybody ought to have a gun*; an addition made by my Mama T. To her way of thinking, if the constitution of the United States says we can, then we shall.

One afternoon, eager to practice with his pump-action pellet gun, baby brother headed out to the woods. What to his wandering eyes did appear, but a mockingbird upon a branch, preening between songs.

My brother's heart raced. He stealthily pumped the gun once, twice, thirty times. He sighted it, pulled the trigger, and POP!

The mockingbird made a muffled thump on the forest floor and my brother stood over it, impressed with his accuracy. Recognizing what he had done, however, and recalling the words of our mother, who counseled him never to shoot an animal he didn't intend to eat, he decided in that instant that a man has to do what a man has to do. So, with hands caked in guilt, he built a fire, gutted and plucked the fowl, shoved the slight body onto a whittled skewer, and roasted it.

"What does that have to do with me," Charlotte scoffed.

Okay, so nothing hair-raising happened to my baby brother, a little kid who acted impulsively, only doing what boys do. I suspect that very likely no ill befell him because he atoned for his transgression by nibbling the unseasoned, gamey meat from the tiny bones of the mockingbird.

Charlotte, on the other hand, a grown woman, (a member of garden club, a lady of confederate heritage), engaged in premeditated sin and, according to her daddy, lawlessness. Good gracious alive, she should know better than to defile and betray the Georgia landscape in such a devil-be-danged manner.

"I guess what I'm trying to tell you, Charlotte," I softly replied, "is you're going to have to eat that tree."

Concrete Flip-Flop

Although every generation has its rules of decorum, mangling magnolias transcends the passage of time. Not to beat the drum to old news, but Charlotte did cut down that magnolia grandiflora from her front yard last year. She defended herself, saying she needed more parking.

In her front yard?

Back in my grandmothers' day, smoking and walking was the tackiest thing a woman could do. Public appearance without lipstick ran a close second. Unlike the lipstick oversight, however, in which pallid lips was the actual error in ways, in the walking and smoking travesty, smoking had nothing to do with the offense.

A woman could sit and smoke until she croaked like a midnight catfish. Not a soul would bat an eye. A woman could chat on the party line while inhaling enough creosote to pave a road from Atlanta to Macon. No one would think the lesser of her. She could even puff while porting carpool, children choking pneumatically in the rear seat. Who would dare accuse her of behaving badly?

But if she took one unvirtuous step toward the grocery store entrance with a tobacco stick squeezed between two fingers, yellowed nails hidden beneath Scarlet Apple polish, the Junior League president would get on the phone with the Garden Club secretary. UDC and DAR would strip the transgressor's membership ribbons from her lapel in the freezer section before she could drop a single TV dinner into her buggy, and the church ladies would ban her lemon squares from the UMW bake sale.

But, for my mother, garishness rooted itself in bare feet. Kids running amuck on summer days dare not darken the door of the supermarket barefoot. Our mamas rightfully feared tuberculosis, the neighbors, or being the subject of deep, determined discussions at Wednesday night prayer group. And TB seemed a far fairer fate than Miss Nell seeing us barefoot on the baked goods aisle, proclaiming us common as creamed corn.

I related all this to Charlotte. "Huh?" she muttered. "What are you talking about?"

Of course, smoking has fallen out of favor and walking has gained strides in the health and fitness world. And the flip-flop, a thin layer of rubber, attached loosely to a big toe by a plastic thong, now holds us on the crumbling edge of respectability. So, good southerners have searched high and low for a new way to distinguish upstanding citizens from undesirables.

"Why'd you cut down that magnolia tree," I judiciously questioned Miss Charlotte.

"So we could have more parking," Charlotte shot back. "You know that."

In the new south, the litmus test for character is the parking of the car. A front yard parker couldn't get an invitation to join the Colonial Dames even if she descended straight from the Jamestown settlers.

"Well we poured a cement pad. We're not just parking on the front lawn or in the dirt," she asserted, offended at my supposed suggestion of impropriety (as if slaying an innocent magnolia hadn't already demonstrated her stance on unwritten rules of etiquette).

"That parking pad of yours," I said to Charlotte, pausing for dramatic effect, "is a concrete flip-flop."

Charlotte looked flabbergasted, but gradually gave me a knowing grin and a nod. She'd ingeniously beaten the southern system, leaving no room for commentary on her pedigree.

Walking and smoking no longer the downfall of genteel living, flip-flops now a fashion staple, it's the parking of the car that will temporarily bring southern civilization to a hallelujah-halt. Untinted lips still run a close second. But the indiscretion of removing a magnolia, my dear Charlotte, may remain a stain "for-eh-vah."

A Fairytale Tornado

Heloise offered Gerta an emergency Ativan, which Gerta politely declined, but perhaps shouldn't have. Such a favor couldn't be more appropriate than when a girl finds herself, pocketbook strap secured over her shoulder, cowering face down under a laundry cart in the bowels of the Ritz Carlton. Although the 11 o'clock news would have us believe differently, tornadoes know no economic boundaries.

Just before they found themselves retreating from the weather, Heloise and Gerta exited the spa giggling and sipping pink champagne. The vast windows in the cavernous lobby framed by towering mahogany timbers revealed a panoramic view of a dark and angry sky. Strikes of thin, pointy lightning, like the claws of a wicked stepmother, snagged the horizon. Hail the size of the Hope Diamond pelted the large veranda. The women watched fearfully, while other oblivious guests appeared determined to make merriment while the Titanic sank.

Heloise, a firm believer that wearing cotton socks and tennis shoes on planes improves chances of running from a fiery crash, and so prides her impeccable focus on the details of survival, dragged Gerta, still holding a champagne glass, up to their 3rd floor quarters. Hustling as fast as two women wearing flip-flops and lavish terrycloth robes can feasibly go with tufts of tissue stuffed between each dainty, pink pedicured toe, they packed their purses full of essential supplies: bottled water, bottled wine, corkscrew, cell phones, changes of underwear, brushes, passports, Town & Country Magazine, lipstick, credit cards.

The ladies opted out of plucking the tissue from their toes and changing into tennis shoes due to the risk of ruining their pedicures. As the recent recipients of Bulgarian massages á la Franz, the tell-tale massage oil still matting their hair, they moved slowly but purposefully back down the stairs to the lobby. Wearing robes and toting overstuffed Versaces slung over their shoulders, these community minded, charitable women tried to convince each person they passed to join them in their flee to the basement.

It was extremely difficult to whip up mayhem, panic, and chaos amongst the weekend revelers. Lightning flashed and the hail increased in carats; but the band played on as the heavens split above paradise. Through concerted effort the ladies finally persuaded a young couple to save themselves from the unfolding catastrophe. Heloise then grabbed a waitress hostage and demanded that she guide the four to safety.

The waitress led them down, down to the lowest level, on a snaking path through the 5-star kitchen to a hallway beyond. And that's where they huddled, Gerta under the laundry cart and Heloise breaking out anti-anxiety remedies. Gerta took to crying. Heloise took the Ativan.

Shortly, Heloise, suddenly chatty, turned to the woman who escaped with them to the basement, and remarked, "Oh, don't you look nice. What a lovely dress you're wearing. When the news crews come, you do the talking for us since you're dressed for the occasion."

Well, the media never came, because neither did the tornado, and after a respectful amount of time, the waitress suggested that they all return to the surface. When I at last got a-hold of Gerta and Heloise to check how they fared the storm, their commandeered waitress, true to the reputation of Ritz Carlton customer service, had rewarded the heroic First Responders with wine spritzers.

Heloise, giddy from her near-death experience, among other things, resolved that from thenceforth she would live life without reserve, AND she vowed to treat me, her dear friend in time of crisis, to a spa-weekend at the Ritz. Natural disasters know no economic boundaries.

Who's Fooling Who?

Greg and his family took a brief summer sojourn to Tybee Island, where they dined out at a little place called Café Loco on the banks of Lazaretto Creek. They sat on the upper deck, which captures the ocean winds rushing inland to meet the marsh breezes and the Savannah River air currents. The last time I myself sat on that deck I spent most of my meal holding down my skirt and pulling my hair out of my lipstick.

Greg's kids ordered baskets of fried Georgia shrimp. Charlotte decided on the stuffed flounder and deviled blue crab combo. Greg, however, ordered Alaskan salmon and a house salad with ranch dressing. In Greg's defense, he probably couldn't think straight for holding down his skirt and keeping his hair out of his lipstick, metaphorically speaking, of course.

Greg's waitress didn't give him the same benefit of the doubt. She went back to the kitchen and yelled, "We've got some yahoo up on the deck who ordered ranch dressing and salmon," to which the dishwasher responded, "Is he a redneck or a sorority girl?" to which the waitress replied, "I couldn't tell. I was holding down my skirt and pulling my hair out of my lipstick."

My Mississippi brother, the space lawyer (if that gives him any additional credibility), counseled me never to order ranch dressing in a dining establishment, because his restauranteur friend, John Tatum, reports that waiters and waitresses say ranch is the dressing of choice among rednecks and sorority girls.

He tells me things like this to prey on my insecurities, to make me think back to the last time I ate ranch dressing in public. He knows I don't want the wait staff to look down on me, and label me, and talk about my food tastes and implied affiliations behind my back.

Greg, on the other hand, is not fazed by snooty servers, even the misguided one who thinks if she tells her whole miserable life story she'll get a bigger tip. After deriding Greg in the kitchen, his waitress returned to refill drinks and proceeded to relate how she could only afford a green Pinto hatchback that ran out of gas on her way to work, because gas is so expensive and she was planning to use that night's tips to fill it up. So she walked the rest of the way in her flip-flops, since her live-in, good-for-nothing boyfriend, Jeremy, who spends all her tips on beer and doesn't have a job and says he won't get one until after the final episode of The Guiding Light airs, wouldn't get off his lazy badonka-donk and rescue her.

So, you see where Greg and the waitress stood with each other. And possibly why, upon delivery of his food, Greg asked her, "Is this salmon local?" causing the waitress to pause with her mouth open and then gush, "Oh, yes sir. It was caught fresh right out there." She pointed toward the creek. "Our chef bought it off the boat this morning."

When she left, Greg told his wife, "Jeremy is never going to get a job."

The waitress announced to the kitchen staff, "That yahoo thinks salmon is local catch from the creek." A ruckus broke out over the sorority girl/redneck wager.

Greg left her a nice tip for being a good sport.

In the end, who fooled who?

I think the lot of us, me, Greg, sorority girls, rednecks, waitresses, maybe you, and especially space lawyers, are all just managing to prevent our skirts from wafting up and our hair from sticking in our lipstick despite the swirl of hot air blowing around us.

Chain of Fools

On the fourth day of an uneventful week at the beach, I lounged at the water's edge. The sun tiptoed across ripples on the horizon, making ships look melty as they approached the north channel of the Savannah River.

Glancing to the southeast, I noticed an erratic yellow dot afloat beyond the breakers. Oddly, it oscillated through phases of slowly rotating vertically and then resting on the surface. This perplexed me.

Nudging Helen, reclined to my left, engrossed in steamy beach reading, I pointed and said, "Look. Do you see that?"

"What," she responded, resisting pulling away just as Lars and Mona met in a breathy, forbidden embrace on the moors, risking discovery, or worse . . .

"Watch. That yellow thing out there will flip and skid."

She watched. I watched. And we both said, "Ooh," as it bounced in the distance.

"It's an inner tube," I suggested.

"Yeah," she agreed.

"It almost looks like someone is trying to get a better grip."

Momentarily forgetting Lars and Mona, Helen added, "It's way out there. He might be in trouble."

Helen tapped my husband. "Look. Do you see that?"

"Yeah."

"What do you think it is?"

"An inner tube that got away."

"No," she insisted. "See how it turns over a few times and stops. Someone is fighting to hold on."

He watched. Helen watched. I watched.

My husband tapped Alan, Helen's spouse. "Look," he said, gesturing. "Do you see that yellow tube out there? There's a man on it who can't swim. There he goes, struggling with it again."

"Man, that guy's in danger," replied Alan.

Alan watched. My husband watched. Helen watched. I watched. Lars and Mona watched.

Vrrrrrmmm. Chatham county lifeguards, conducting routine beach patrol, approached on a four wheeler. I waved them down and the four of us hastened to tell about the live bait adrift in the oceanic food chain.

The lifeguards looked. We looked. Lars and Mona looked. Bystanders looked.

Caught up in our heroism, we offered our services. Alan volunteered his medical expertise. My husband proposed to walk the beach seeking out the fellow's widow and orphans. Helen and I served the muscular, tanned lifeguards refreshments. Lars and Mona paused their personal drama.

Chsh-chsh-chsh-chsh-chsh-chsh. More lifeguards arrived on jet skis. The yellow tube had diminished to a dot on the radar, and the jet ski coalition appeared to search in vain for the casualty.

Thmp-thmp-thmp-thmp-thmp. They called in the Coastguard. Coastguard helicopters and boats scoured the salty vault.

As the search continued through the afternoon, a disappointed Alan declared, "A botched operation."

"Yeah," my husband agreed. "They'll never find him now."

"Shark chum for sure," I chimed in.

Later that evening, I phoned the Coastguard station. "Yes, ma'am," I presumptuously greeted the operator, "I reported that poor fellow on a yellow inner tube swept out in the Atlantic today. Did they recover the body?"

After a brief pause, she spoke.

"Mm-hm," I responded. "Mm-hm. Yes ma'am. Okay. I see. Well, I guess that's that. No, I don't care to give you my name for the official report." Click.

The team recovered the inner tube. No one was with it and no swimmers were reported missing. Since the whole blankety-blank lot of them was out there searching for a yellow herring, they used it as a joint training exercise. I cost the feds a lot of money.

This news stunned my husband. It stunned me. It stunned Helen and Alan. And it stunned Lars and Mona, who, subsequently re-entwined, and resumed tempting fate . . .

Value of a L(W)ife

What is the value of a l(w)ife? An acquaintance went to a life insurance salesman and requested a policy with an $800,000 payout to her family in case of her untimely death. To gage her insurability, the examiner asked a few routine questions:

"How old are you?"

"36"

"Marital status?"

"Married."

"How many children?"

"Four."

"How would you rate your health?"

"Mental or physical?"

"Both"

"Physically, excellent. My mental health fluctuates, depending on the situation and the day, but I'm not dangerous to myself or others. I sometimes raise my voice and flail my arms, that's all."

The insurance salesman nodded his head, made a check mark at certifiably crazy and forged ahead, "Your occupation?"

"Housewife and full-time mom."

He erased the check mark next to Certifiably Crazy and put it next to Mentally Challenged. Then he said, "Ma'am, you don't need a policy this big."

"Yes, I do," Christie insisted.

"No Ma'am, you don't. Only people who add value to a family need life insurance in this amount."

Christie sat there, stunned. She could feel her chest flushing and red splotches spreading up her neck to her cheeks. Flustered, she got up to leave, but stopped. She turned around to face the guy, now shuffling papers on his desk. "Let me tell you my value," she said.

Before he could protest, she began: "My work day starts at 5:30am. I crack eggs and make coffee. In my head I keep track of which child eats his bagel with jelly and no butter, which has a bagel with butter and no jelly, who likes it with cream cheese and grape, but not apple, jam, and who wants one with peanut butter on the side.

I scramble the eggs not too soft and not too hard with three pieces of cheese in half the eggs and one piece in the other half.

I put my John Hancock on folders, notes, papers and planners for my school-age children, prepare individualized lunches, stuff backpacks and hustle everyone out to the car. After dropping two children off at elementary school, I return home to dress the others.

Then I get back in the car and take the preschooler to his class, drive home again and change the youngest's diaper.

Four loads of clothes, eight puzzles, forty toddler's questions and two clean bathrooms later, it's noon and I retrieve the four year-old. We return home, where I make more child-specific lunches, eat three potato chips myself and put the kids down for a nap.

I do additional laundry, clean the kitchen, mop the floor, plan a menu, write a grocery list and make dentist appointments. Then I juggle money, pay bills and wake up pit vipers from deep sleep so I can get the other two from school.

We go to the post office, the dry cleaners and the grocery store. I haul four children in and out of the car, shopping carts and display racks. Back at home, I unload the car, put the groceries away, supervise homework, break up fights, and concoct a meal in which no two single food items touch each other."

Here, Christie inhaled, preparing to continue her rant. Mr. Insurance Man saw his opening, "Your husband is a very lucky man to have a wife who takes such good care of him."

"Oh," said Christie, "Would you like to know what I do for my husband?"

Not wanting to go there, the man granted my friend her insurance policy. He also erased the check mark next to Mentally Challenged and put it next to Thinks Outside the Box.

Paige Helps

You know what happens when you help someone. You end up helping over and over again - Paige believes this. But Paige is a good soul. She helps anyway.

As Paige stood looking out the plate-glass window at the Family Y, waiting for participants in her soon-to-start aerobics class to arrive, a woman in an electric wheelchair towing a shopping cart cruised toward the busy, four-lane highway. Paige's exercise outfit got in a bind. Clad in red leotard and white aerobics shoes, sans cape, Paige ran out and yelled, "STOP! You can't cross that street by yourself!"

"Oh, no, ma'am, I'm just cutting through this parking lot and heading up that hill behind those buildings." The buggy, full of large cans of grape juice, several bottles of Sprite, and packages of raw chicken, looked wobbly. Paige knew the handicapped shopper would never make it.

Her spandex outfit shining brilliantly in the afternoon sun, Paige insisted on pushing the cart up the hill. When the uncommon pair neared the top, the woman asked Paige to help her unload everything from the cart into the wheelchair. "How will you carry all this stuff like that?" Paige protested.

"Aw, girl, let's see. You can fit about three cans of that juice on each one o' these footrests." The lady grunted and heaved and lifted one leg at a time and Paige, because she couldn't think of an alternative solution, shoved the cans into place.

"Now put those Sprites right here on my lap."

"How are you going to reach the controls if I do that?" a perplexed Paige asked.

"I got it child. Don't worry 'bout me." So Paige, against her better judgment, stacked on the 2-liter bottles and hung the bags of chicken from the handles.

The woman eased off, vvvMmmm, vvMMmmm, maneuvering the chair over the bumpy terrain, plastic sacks of raw meat swinging. But when she picked up speed, two wheels lifted, tilting the driver at a precarious angle. Again, Paige yelled, "STOP!"

"I tell you what," a flustered Paige hurried over and suggested, "I'll hide your grape juice and Sprite over in those woods. You go home and get someone to come back and help you." Also rattled from the near calamity, the woman agreed, again gasping and choking as she held her legs aloft. Paige removed the cans of juice and carried them over to the thick brush.

Finally free from her Good Samaritan obligation, Paige turned and dashed back to the Family Y, her slick red leotard and leggings flashing.

Forty-five minutes later, Paige lay supine on the gym floor, leading stomach crunches, ". . . nine, ten, hold it, and relax. Again, one, two, hold it . . ." The door flew open and a pair of legs agilely stomped right up next to Paige's ear.

Confused, Paige looked up and tried to put it all together while the hysterical, towering female pointed and screamed, "You go tell that man I did not steal anything! He says I stole it! You go tell him it's mine!"

"Okay, okay," Paige replied, as it all meshed. And she followed the running woman up the hill. Paige, her tight, red, superhero, spandex aerobics outfit glistening in the sun, dutifully explained to the frowning proprietor of the optometrist's office, standing in his rear parking lot with his arms crossed, about how she had helped this woman, previously confined to a wheelchair, hide the drinks in the woods.

Not only that, but Paige fulfilled her do-gooder duty by making the man apologize for accusing the miraculously healed woman of stealing.

Help once. Help again. Paige will.

Garden Club

Heloise and I met downtown to do what women do best: Talk. This night we sipped pilsners of Rogue Dead Guy and exchanged stories that would stir him, and my grandmothers, from the grave.

Every southern township, worth its weight in tomatoes, has a garden club; or, as my girlfriends often slip into saying, garden club. Since the advent of the working mother, many such organizations have long gone grey; thus, the flourish of recruitment efforts to snag more supple branches. That's how Heloise got involved in The Society of the Sisters of the Lily, participating in projects like decorating birdhouses, hats, and pocket books to resemble mini Rose Bowl floats.

Her favorite part of meetings, nonetheless, is watching as the delicate ladies of the sorority of the flower politely, yet pointedly, throw verbal pyracanthus thorns at each other's backs. "It's priceless," she chortles, "when the white gloves come off."

That is precisely why you can never breathe a word of the following story Heloise confidentially shared with me. I, myself, at the telling, giggled so hard my mug shattered. Rogue Dead Guy bled all over the table.

Several months ago, on Heloise's assigned pettifore day, her child presented with an oozing wound requiring immediate medical attention. As the club's by-laws clearly state, however, members unable to fulfill their duties must notify the snack committee chairwoman, vice president of affairs, and corresponding secretary. With only thirty minutes to meeting time, she called Mrs. Betty Anne Renfrowe and reported the dire circumstances in which she found herself.

"Well, you do have your dessert prepared," Betty Anne asserted.

There are two things about southern women: First, we exude unruffled perfection in all tasks, large or small, regardless of our circumstances.

Therefore, Heloise lied, "Yes."

Secondly, the better half of the south will die a martyr's death before putting on the face of impoliteness.

Betty Anne replied, "I'll swing by on my way, deah. Don't worry about a thing."

Wrapping another towel around her child's gushing gash, Heloise dutifully waited. This gave Heloise just enough time to think about crawling into the freezer and closing the door.

Instead, she sensibly pulled strawberries from the fridge, sliced them, arranged them on a crystal tray, and snatched a few mint leaves from an herb planter for garnish. The only thing missing was dip. She had no powdered sugar.

Not to fret. Two generations younger than most matrons in garden club, she happened to have certain supplies on hand. Things that, shall I say, make life a little sweeter.

From the farthest corner of the top shelf of her pantry, she pulled out a jar of deliciously tantalizing chocolate body paint. She'd been saving it for a special occasion.

Setting aside the accompanying paintbrush, she carefully poured the contents of the jar into a crystal bowl placed in the center of the berries. Just as Betty Anne let herself in with a, "Yoohoo, I'm heah," Heloise whisked the tell-tale container and brush out of sight.

Later, Betty Anne called to say how much the ladies of the Lily enjoyed the fare. "We all simply tittered with delight. Miss Cicily had seconds and thirds and all the girls want to know your recipe for au chocolate. I don't think we've evah had such a grand time judging the plant samples befoah."

Heloise and I flagged down our waitress and each ordered another Rogue Dead Guy brought to our table. Through uncontrollable laughter I quipped, "So they really got sauced."

"Dahlin," she rejoined, "they were happiah than cockroaches on a pop-taht."

Friends on the North End

"**S**o, let's get the tour over with," she said, when we entered her home.

"The tour?" I hadn't realized this budding island friendship came with a tour.

"Yes," she replied. "I know you want to see the house, so let's get it done, and then we'll have drinks on the veranda."

"I think I'll take my drink now." A beverage in my hand might prevent me from putting a foot in my mouth.

Our hostess explained, to her presumed neophytes, "They call this area Captain's Row, because ship captains lived here." Unfortunately, I didn't lift my glass fast enough to stop "No duh" from slipping across my lips.

Undaunted, she traipsed us up and down her stairs, meanwhile enlightening us on the fringe benefits of her job in a plastic surgeon's office. Flicking first her buttocks and then her breasts, she assured us, "Next year you'll see a little less of this and a little more of that."

I desperately wanted to inquire if it would be a transplant, even though I couldn't tell much about her figure hidden under a green ki-mumu whatchacallit (according to our docent, a style all the rage in Vogue). But I refrained, because no amount of rearranging body parts could make a woman appealing in a mu-nono.

Finally, she led us onto the front porch to enjoy our cocktails and the ocean breeze. "What do you do," she thoughtfully asked.

When I explained I write a newspaper column, she ran inside and exited again, shoving a book at me. "You must read it. This lady does just what you do, except she's a little more successful. I tell you, she's sitting on the cheddar."

Gee, thanks. But really, I prefer to bumble along in euphoria, thinking I work in an uncharted niche. And sitting on the cheddar, is that the same as cutting the cheese? Alas the breeze ceased and the no-see-ums appeared (rather large and hungry), and someone suggested we go to dinner. My new acquaintance, in the most agreeable manner, said, about herself and her spouse, "We're flexible as long as we stay on the North end of the island." How congenial of them. I guess, quarantining themselves, they never noticed that on a four mile island, the north end and the south end are practically the same.

Finally, we agreed upon a restaurant within the required radius of their home. I looked forward to another drink, a leisurely meal in the arms of the old fort, and light banter among friends.

Shortly after receiving my appetizer, however, I realized that geisha girl's eyes were boring into me. I looked up.

"Are you enjoying your crab cakes," she pleasantly inquired.

"Yes. They're delicious. Would you care to try a bite?"

"No," she said, urgently. "Are you almost finished? I need to use the restroom."

"The bathroom is just inside that door and to the left," I cheerfully informed her.

"Oh, I don't use public facilities," she said, and visibly recoiled.

I had used the restaurant's public loo twice while in her company. But in her defense, maybe she needed to drop some of that cheddar she was sitting on.

At any rate, since I know our new friends won't travel beyond the reach of their shower head, I look forward to our next island sabbatical, putting on my best flip-flops, inviting them over to Hoping for a Hurricane Hideaway, giving a tour of our single-wide by the sea, and entertaining on the redwood deck.

. . . All within pottying distance of their house.

HDL and LDL and Little Lambs Eat Ivy

Two precious little girls live down the street from me, and as I am skittish to name names or spell out initials, I shall identify them, as all southern belles are identified, on everything from napkins to toilet lids, by their monograms.

They are sisters, the older one's monogram aptly being HDL and the younger one's quite correctly being LDL. I oft affectionately refer to them as Good Cholesterol and Bad Cholesterol. Which leads to that age-old cholesterol question: Should we elevate the good or just learn to live with the bad?

Little Miss Good Cholesterol frequently comes over to play amiably with my daughter, age six. Little Miss Bad Cholesterol tags along because I feel guilty inviting only the older sister and leaving the younger at home. In the beginning she made it her mission to interfere in the older girls' princess play, but, having grown intensely bored with that, she now happily hangs with me. She must sense that I am so much like her, unredeemably b-a-d.

And while Little Miss Good Cholesterol, Miss HDL, is so very, very good - she loves for me to paint her fingernails and never complains about the color - Little Miss Bad Cholesterol, Miss LDL, well, you can probably guess. She's never satisfied with the color. And she's always "hongwy," which she says in her thick four year-old voice, for whatever snacks I might have, especially my secret chocolate stash.

And if I feed her, she only comes back, her appetite piqued, saying, "Miss Lucy, I'm still hongwy." But I do love that LDL like I love a chocolate-coated fried Twinkie, maybe better; which makes it completely forgivable when she brings me a crinkling plastic baggie, a chocolate ring around her puckered mouth, saying, "Miss Lucy, you're out of these." Her left hand slapped smack dab on her hip, she takes on a perturbed tone, unabashedly irritated that I would let someone eat all the chocolate chips, even if it was her, because now there are none, and by golly, she's "still hongwy."

I have her come over at least once a week, 'cause she's happy enough simply following me around my house spilling her family's secrets. Oh, and what a mess! She drops tiny tidbits like, "Miss Lucy, you gotta dead woach on the floor over there." Then while I'm sweeping it up, she adds, "My house has more woaches than your house."

Feeding her four year-old train of thought, I say something like, "Well, darn. I guess y'all win that contest."

"We do," she insists matter-of-factly. "And ours are all awive."

Just this past Sunday, Bad Cholesterol came on over with HDL, and while Good Cholesterol and my daughter played dress-up, LDL brushed my hair, helped me fold clothes, and sidekicked around with me to put away clean laundry. "You're nicer than my mama," she blurted out.

I egged her on, "Why do you say that?"

"My mama won't let us have dessert every night," she tattled.

"I don't let my children have dessert every night either. They hardly ever get dessert." I felt truthfulness, despite risking the loss of a naïve child's undying devotion, was best here.

"You're still nicer than my mama."

Now, if I never did before, I see the allure of Bad Cholesterol and why folks find it so hard to give up. 'Cause while HDL never gets into my chocolate stash and always agrees with me, I can sure swill on the fat lies LDL butters me up with. And like all things southern, including cholesterol, anyone would certainly recognize her by her monogram.

Squirrel's Afire

Maynard checked his TAB colas in the bottom drawer of the fridge. He righted one, wondering how it flipped since the last time he assessed the cans, five minutes before.

Seeing my consternation, Maynard's stepbrother whispered, "We just like to have a little fun with him. He drinks TAB like fish drink water, and he keeps the cans arranged just-so. We move a can here and again, to shake things up."

When I glanced at him disparagingly, he defended himself, saying, "If we didn't, what would Maynard have to look forward to when he checked the drawer?"

Obviously, Maynard, a forty-five year-old bagboy, who refuses to sack rice with potatoes because of a supposed conflict of interest, is off the chain. But I soon learned the entire family's teakettle isn't whistling.

Smiling warily at my host, I followed him to the den, where his dad busied himself building a fire. The warm Savannah winter had relegated two chords of wood on the pool patio to rot. So, when the temperature finally dipped to forty-five degrees, these folks salvaged the kindling.

My friend's father, laying logs in an antagonizingly meticulous manner, approached fire making like Michelangelo approached painting the Sistine Chapel; this gave Maynard three more opportunities to tend his TABs. Meanwhile, the lady of the house nagged, "Honey, haven't you finished yet?" followed by asking, "Do y'all hear that noise?"

"That's just Maynard shifting cans in the produce drawer," said my host.

"If I've told you once, I've told you a thousand times, stop agitating that boy." Then she paused and cocked her head like a hound on a coon hunt. "There it is again. Do y'all hear that?"

By now, a thin string of smoke wafted up the chimney and the patriarch, a surgeon of soot, barked out commands for more paper, more wood and more lighter fluid - the accoutrements of disaster. And since I now stood passing anything potentially flammable over the shoulder of a man I'd only met an hour earlier, I started to hear things myself. But, fearing that Maynard and I were both being played for fools, I kept quiet.

Breezing back into the room, my friend's stepmother exclaimed, "Good gracious, it's getting louder. Surely you all can hear it."

A crackling inferno wildly whipped up the chimney, and the master stood proudly with poker in hand, his primitive instinct fulfilled.

Briefly content, Maynard sat on the sofa. My host temporarily exited to twist TABs. And his stepmother stood next to me declaring, "I hear something. It's scratching, scratching, scratching. I can't stand it." She pressed her hands on her ears to obstruct the tell-tale heart.

Quite suddenly, the disturbance became audible to all. Every eye turned to the fireplace as the scritch-scratch chorused with a squealing and scrambling duet.

Seconds later, a black blaze shot out of the fire and up the man holding the poker. Primal impulses now told him to drop the iron and scream like a schoolgirl.

We yelped and dodged, while the screeching fireball slid across the mantel, climbed the curtains, leapt to the sofa, and ran a dramatic, unpredictable, zig-zag course through the room, flames flagging, leaving a labyrinth of damage behind. "Dadgum," someone bellowed, "that squirrel's afire!"

(Maynard tormented over whether to check his TABs.)

Culminating in a horrific scene, as quickly as the excitement began, it died. On a circle of singed carpet lay the charred remains, toenails glowing, tail still twitching. A morose silence hung over us.

"Um," the stepbrother cleared his throat, "I guess the little guy won't move your TABs anymore, Maynard."

Thump, Thump, Thump, Thump . . . Thump

My friend Jane-Ann stood in her front yard, near the sidewalk, watering her zinnias last Saturday, when along down Zenana Street strolled her new neighbor, Francis. Jane-Ann and Francis had never seen the interiors of each other's homes; nor had they ever bonded on a zig-zagging trip across town to the emergency room with a screaming toddler in the backseat. The number of deep, intimate conversations ever shared amounted to zero.

General neighborhood rules provide for sidewalk acquaintances to give shallow salutations paired with polite hand waves. Brief conversations about one another's rogue sprinkler heads spraying the street, or Zoodle the poodle pooping under feet, may transpire, but go no further. Thus, peace and civility reign supreme in suburbia.

Last Saturday, Jane-Ann smiled as Francis zipped toward her, clipping along swiftly. Out of breath when she reached Jane-Ann, Francis stopped and sat on the stoop.

Jane-Ann kept watering the zinnias and asked, "How's it going?"

"Oh, fine," said Francis. "I'm trying to get in shape, lose a little weight, get rid of the shift and drift, if you know what I mean."

Sizing up Francis, and noting that a pack of wild dogs would pass her by thinking the buzzards had already picked her bones clean, Jane-Ann said, "I don't think you need to lose any weight. You look great. Whatever shifted and drifted must have fallen off when you came buzzing around the corner at Zimmerman Way."

This got Francis's zodiac up. "Well if you had a husband and a horoscope like mine, you wouldn't say that. Under my sign in the newspaper today, it said, 'Beware the unexpected. Time changes people. Do what you can to change with him.'"

"Huh?"

"And Zack is an unbelievably difficult man to live with. He never spends any time at home. He takes every extra work shift he can get. And you wouldn't believe the zingers he zooms at me. He says I'm fat, stupid, lazy, neurotic, nervous, naggy, needy, silly, and senseless. The last time I remember him smiling was the day before he quit smoking, twenty years ago. I can't cook, sew, keep the house clean enough, or wash the clothes right. I have failed as a wife."

Jane-Ann, unprepared for this emotional outpouring on the neighborhood byways, stood agape in her zinnias, the hose watering her numb feet. What a jerk, she thought. She wondered what to say, how to comfort this near stranger seeking solace on her doorstep.

Meanwhile, Francis prattled on about the mediocrity of her fading existence.

Turning off the spigot, Jane-Ann leaned in and spoke confidentially to Francis, who did not stop talking. Jane-Ann offered a plan.

She suggested that Francis, at approximately 5:50am on Monday, station herself in the cranked car in the driveway, with the radio blaring. According to Jane-Ann, everything would go smoother if Francis also sang at the top of her lungs.

"Are you listening Francis? I'm helping you out here," said Jane-Ann. But Francis now discussed how wretchedly her children behave in public, even when she gives them treats.

"Now, when your husband walks down to get the morning paper, you throw the car in reverse, press the gas, don't look back, and don't stop until you hear a thump."

Francis rang her hands, and droned on about how her mother criticizes her.

Jane-Ann caught up in her creativity, recanted, "No make that 2 thumps, for insurance. Actually, three to four thumps, because it will only look like an accident if you pull forward again and get out to see what you hit."

Childhood memories for Francis also seeped slippery self-pity. She just didn't understand why her father never brought her presents home from work to make her feel special.

Still directing instructions to the guest at the pity party, Jane-Ann said, "And when you go to investigate the thumps, leave the car in neutral."

"Oh thank you, for letting me go on like that," said Francis, standing to go. "What you were saying?"

"Oh nothing, just I think I'm going to pull those zinnias out."

An evil mind is a terrible thing to waste.

Chapter Five

Almost Famous

One morning at circle time, when a fellow teacher announced the title of the story she planned to read, a little girl blurted, "I hate the five little ducklings. I hope Fox eats them this time so we can hear another story tomorrow."

A classmate, diligently sitting criss-cross applesauce looked horrified and started to squirm. "What's wrong," asked the teacher.

"Mama says we don't say butt, hate, or damn at school."

Going to the Dogs

Dog lovers act crazy about their steadfast companions. And humanizing these animals has expanded into an American pastime, with people indulging their dogs with jewel studded collars and doggy buffet tables. Many of us tag our dogs with people names, like Max or Sam, and then talk to them like they understand every word, even allowing them the opportunity to respond.

Taking it up a notch, some canine owners tote their pets in purse-like baby carriers, and allow their dogs to sleep in the bed and eat off of their plates at the table. In my mind these individuals tread awfully close to the edge of madness, maybe with one foot actually slipping off the rim; but they have yet to go wholly over the cliff, pooch in purse and all.

The dog owners who actually have skidded into insanity throw their dogs birthday parties, elevating the beasts from man's best friend to babes in arms; which brings me to a true, but tragic tale, of a birthday party gone to the dogs.

Sheila, the proud owner of Mitzi, a shiatsu on the crest of her second birthday, decided to honor the toddler. *Mitzi, who is turning two/ would be pleased if you/ would come to help her celebrate/ with doggy games and special cake,* read the invitation, which I regret to report was indiscriminately sent to all of Mitzi's "friends."

On party day, eight guests arrived at two o'clock: two poodles, one English bulldog mix, one golden retriever, one Chihuahua, one Chihuahua-shiatsu mix, and two chocolate lab brothers. As each guest arrived, a cone shaped party hat was placed on its head and strapped behind the ears. The tight elastic of the party hats, combined with all the sniffing going on, elevated the excitement in the atmosphere.

The agenda included party games like drool on the sofa until the color fades, bark 'til you drop, and tear the cat piñata to shreds. All of the merrymaking, particularly the piñata fun, led to a fierce appetite among the party guests. Despite telling Cujo several times to stop bearing his teeth and gums at Lupe (who was bearing his teeth and gums at the chocolate lab brothers), Sheila felt Mitzi's party was proceeding quite well.

It came time to serve the cake, so all the guests were seated in their chairs (yes, chairs) around the table (yes, a table) with Mitzi at the head. Before Sheila brought out the cake, Mitzi opened her presents: a new squeak toy that sounded distinctly like a taunting squirrel, a variety pack of sumptuous dog treats in beef, chicken, and pork flavors, two chew bones, three tug of war ropes, and one synthetic raccoon tail on a string, infused with raccoon scent.

The polite guests dared not play with the birthday girl's new toys, and remained in their seats quivering and salivating as "Happy Birthday to Mitzi" was joyously sung. Afterwards, the cake (a delicious bakery cake) was cut and Mitzi, because she was the honored birthday dog, received the first piece.

Poor Mitzi, she never hand a chance. Her birthday, her birthday cake, and Mitzi too, I'm afraid, all went to the dogs.

When Sheila recounted this story with tears in her eyes, showing pictures of the party right up to Mitzi's demise, the lesson in it occurred to her: Your own dog might be human, but that doesn't mean her friends are.

POP!

You may never have heard of Neil Tillotson until now. It amazes me that the man who inflicted one of the worst scourges ever endured by families never gained more notoriety amongst the American public.

Had he not died in 2001 at age one hundred and two (his longevity likely due to dealings with the devil), I would give the old man an ear horn full of "Waaaah."

To extract payment for his atrocious offense, I would lock him in a room with 10 preschoolers, 9 balloons, and 25 foot ceilings. Even novice mathematicians know that equation equals disaster.

Mr. Tillotson, were he able from the grave, might argue that he invented the latex balloon during the Great Depression . . . to cheer people. I dispute that point with one word – foreshadowing.

Balloons, particularly ones filled with helium, make children happy, enthralled, joyful, even mystified . . . shortly before they trigger wails, sobs, moans, and mourning. These air-filled bulbs of bafflement pin-ball youngsters back and forth between vast, emotional extremes, with their weary guardians chasing.

Where fascination ends, and it always ends, loud, inconsolable grieving begins. Sometimes just facing the fact that he can't have the green balloon, because Johnny in line in front of him got it, sends a toddler to the floor, legs and arms aflail.

Other times a tot dribbles tears when mother, imbued with the God-given ability to see eight minutes into the future, suggests tying the string attached to the tenuous treasure to the child's wrist. Exasperated, she gives up and hands the string to the whiner, thrilling him beyond giddy foot stamping.

Just like Mama knew he would, little Ned lets go . . . and it's gone.

So now the youngster yelps, staring up at the ceiling, or worse the sky, watching his balloon get smaller. With his face wet and red and his upper lip sticky from a runny nose, he reaches two pudgy hands over his head in desperation; the whole time glancing from the object of his desire to Daddy, as if to say, I thought you could do anything.

Foolish parents, wishing to squelch the atmosphere of anguish, get the kid another balloon. All the way home, dad drives with it obstructing the rearview mirror, hitting him on the back of the head, poomp, poomp, and rubbing static electricity into his hair. Glee envelops the backseat.

Arriving home, the cheerful child hops out of the car. The balloon, now secured tightly to his wrist, trails somewhere behind.

Wham! POP! Whaaahhhhh!; thus closes the door on contentment. This time Ned cries twice as hard; some because the POP! scared the be-geezers out of him, and more because, well, the balloon is gone, again.

His mama yanks the slobbery remains out of his mouth while he tries to blow air back into them, speaking sternly to him of the dangers of the limp latex she insisted on triple knotting to his arm.

Truly, it's good that things happened this way. It prevented the bal-loon-in-the-ceiling-fan-in-the-middle-of-the-night ordeal. It waylaid the my-balloon-doesn't-float-anymore-make-it-go-up trials the following morning. It circumvented more blubbering.

But not forever. Little ones bawl over balloons because no matter their past experiences, maybe as a result of, they always want another, and they know that one is never enough.

If I got Mr. Tillotson into that room, I would lace the ceiling with nee-dles, grease the fingers of all ten children with baby oil, coach them to beg for the only blue balloon, and assure them they can each have two. That way he could appreciate the full impact of the great depression.

Trouble

Sometimes we go looking for trouble. Sometimes trouble comes looking for us. And sometimes we deliberately bring trouble into our homes . . .

Quite by accident, while dining out, I overheard a careful conversation between a husband and a wife. Always on the prowl for a story, I covertly leaned closer to accurately capture the essence, as well as each word, of what they whispered.

"I'm at my wits' end," the woman said. "Trouble is on the loose everyday and sits in the doorway, where I get my feet tangled in it."

Scooting my chair nearer to hear better, it scraped across the floor, and they both looked at me. I mouthed "Sorry," and feigned looking for my fork under the table.

When things settled down, the man replied to his wife, sympathetically, "I know, I know. I nearly ran into Trouble backing out of the driveway yesterday. I wonder if the neighbors are seeing trouble."

"Probably more than we think," said his companion. "Mr. Dempsey, two doors down, told me he had to ward Trouble off with a broom while rolling down his garage door. And Trouble managed to squeeze in anyway."

By now I was truly intrigued. The whole tale resonated with a Stephen King quality – some intangible entity nicknamed Trouble terrorizes the townsfolk in an otherwise cloistered and innocent community. Before I knew it, I murmured, a little louder than I should have, "Ch-ching, jackpot."

The couple turned and looked at me, startled that we nearly knocked noses. Without them noticing, I had crept not only my chair, but my entire table so close to theirs that the two were virtually seamless. I avoided eye contact, however, and fumbled in my purse for a notepad.

"Anyway," said the wife, speaking now in a low mumble, while eyeing me writing furiously, "last Saturday, Trouble jolted out of the ditch, knocked Abby on her face and left muddy tracks across her back. We barely made it to the house before Trouble returned. Trouble, it turns out, was chasing Mischief."

"Is Mischief okay?" asked her ally.

"And today Trouble dragged Andrew down the street," she continued, without pause, "causing a gash in his leg . . . Honey, Trouble is unpredictable. I really think we must do something."

Unable to contain myself any longer, and picturing a neighborhood lynch mob carrying torches through the night, determined to rid their town of Trouble, I spoke up in my most congenial voice. "It sounds like Trouble follows you wherever you go."

Naturally, they stared at me, a stranger, sitting in their personal space and now barging into their intimate exchange. But the lady of the house finally said, "Trouble has a crimp in its tail where I slammed it in the door."

"Wow," I responded, nodding and taking notes, "sounds like you've had a lot of close calls with Trouble. What do you plan to do?"

Inspiration lit up the eyes of my female counterpart. "Hey," she asked, in a confidential, yet menacing, tenor, "do you want Trouble?"

"Yeah," her husband agreed. "You look like you could use a little Trouble. And how about Mischief, too," he added, glancing stealthily at his wife for approval.

Scared and stammering, "N-n-n-n-o-o-o-o," I clumsily stood and attempted, with difficulty, to drag my table and chair away.

"What's the matter," they taunted, "you're not a *dog* person?"

Momentarily, the waitress arrived, "Will this be on one ticket or two?"

"One," I exclaimed and grabbed it, hoping to bribe my way out of Mischief and Trouble.

Falling for Teacher

"I think you better get out of that hobby, while you can still walk away from it," my uncle admonished his friend, Richard. "I saw on the news where a guy went nose down in one of those contraptions the other day. Crashed and burned."

"Naah," said Richard, affectionately patting his machine, "This is my baby. Besides, I know what I'm doing. I've got one of the best instructors around."

Richard flies an ultralight plane through the skies of rural Edgefield County.

Rich assembled his ultralight plane in his garage using snap-together aluminum tube and fabric. The kit came via UPS in a cardboard box. Although many manufacturers sell engines and assembly services for an additional cost, Richard opted out of those expensive add-ons, grumbling about fools falling for sales gimmicks. Following the simple instructions, he put together his wings with a hot glue gun, twist ties, and an iron.

Why an iron, one might ask? Well, number one, self-assemblers pray over it while getting wrinkles out of the control surfaces, and number two, pilots use it as an in-flight safety system. When the engine cuts, they knock themselves unconscious, in hopes of dieing without soiling their britches first.

On the advice of his teacher, Richard reworked an old motor, from a lawnmower he cast aside years before because it choked out constantly. His wife, Mertice, recalls him kicking it and screaming that it wasn't any better than a seeing-eye dog behind the wheel of a monster truck. With a change of heart, considering previous slurs against the pull-motor just grass in the bag, Richard strapped it to the fragile frame.

If anyone is wondering, an ultralight plane and a glider are not one and the same. Enthusiasts like Richard make a clear distinction. Inferior gliders depend on another pilot in another aircraft to loft them. Ultralight planes, the owners smugly argue, have engines and, thus, real pilots who independently surge their vehicles to flight.

On the other hand, there's a caveat. A glider will stay afloat on air currents, usually until the so-called pilot decides to land. Ultralights, however, will not hover, float, drift or otherwise remain airborne without the steady whir of a gas powered motor. Once the weed eater string tangles, an ultralight turns south like a Canadian goose in September.

Richard and his fellow aviators possess clear enthusiasm for Russian roulette.

Last week, after frugally patching holes in his fuselage fabric with worn out dishtowels from his wife's rag basket, Richard's instructor took his blender powered sky basket for a test-spin around the pasture. Abruptly, the motor noise changed from humming, to zinging, to plinking. Then it quit making noise altogether. That's when he grabbed the iron and started cussing himself for not sewing together a parachute from old bed sheets.

Richard called my uncle yesterday. "I just can't believe it," he lamented. "Mertice says I've got to give up flying."

"She's right, but why did she say that," asked my uncle.

"I don't have an instructor anymore."

"Oh?"

"Yeah, his wife hit pay dirt in that field behind Jubral McGruder's barn. Mac had to send one of his cows that got hit with the shrapnel to the packing plant. But I told Mertice this is just a sign," continued Richard.

Exasperated with this nonsense, my uncle questioned him, "A sign? A sign of what? A sign that, if you couldn't swim, you would take up boating in a craft that wouldn't float unless the propeller turned?"

"No," he dismissed my uncle, exuberantly explaining, "A sign that the student has become the teacher."

Almost Famous

Cookie Hogan. What a name! It rings of the adventurous heroine of my girlhood, Pippy Longstockings. Cookie Hogan should never have lived her life as an average kid in the burbs of Savannah.

With a name like that, she could have traveled the wilds of South America in a 40-foot river boat that she paddled up stream by herself, visiting primitive peoples wearing index finger bones through their noses, riding Shetland ponies, and offering shrunken wild boar heads as tokens of welcome.

Her spellbinding autobiography of her over-the-top exploits with the pygmy barbarians of the Peedon Yellow Mountains in the flatlands of Patagonia, properly titled, The Unbelievable, but Possibly True, Adventures of Cookie Hogan, would have made the New York Times Bestseller List, if only she had discerned the possibilities in her name.

Cookie, you were almost famous.

Unfortunately, lots of people, with notable names, regrettably slip through the cracks of distinction. They fail to recognize the marketing potential of their monikers. Take Happy Jet, for instance, who attended camp with me for summers on end. She wore her hair in a "cute" little bob and "cutely" bounced on her toes wherever she walked. For five years running, to my chagrin, she won the Best Camper award; a résumé builder for sure.

And, as if all that didn't stack her deck, her parents rigged her birth certificate for future success, too. Her name alone would suffice as collateral on a bank loan to support her investment in a discount airline. "You go get 'em girl," the bank president would shout, as she waltzed out of his vault with a billion unsecured dollars to prop her up in a shaky industry.

After all, who wouldn't want to fly a Happy Jet?

In real life Buster Ash sells insurance in Rome, Georgia. By the looks of his office, he does well. But, I bet he would give the actuaries the finger for a chance to see the headline, "Buster Ash, World Renowned Attorney to the Cuckold, Wins Big." Money would run through the hands of jilted husbands, like warm grits through a slotted spoon, as they desperately paid millions to Mr. Ash for his severance services. Women around the world would cover their ***es (rhymes with glasses) at the sheer mention of his name.

Don't forget Rock Hart, candidate for sheriff of Franklin County, who lives with a built-in political slogan: Nothing Scares a Criminal Like a

"Hart" of Stone . . . Vote Rock Hart for Franklin County Sheriff. Climbing the crime fighting ladder requires a hardened heart, and that's a campaign sticking point. Unfortunately, the campaign cache hit rock bottom, and his signs, sitting in groupings of professional self-promotion banners, suffered hand-painting on ragged trapezoidal shaped plywood; so much for visions of himself as head of Homeland Security. Woulda', coulda', shoulda' . . .

Finally, my favorite. Imagine if Weatherly Summers, mild mannered housewife of Dacula, Georgia, had, instead of seeking a husband, sought a double major in meteorology and communications. The whole nation would tune in to hear her announce the climate conditions on the Today Show each weekday morning. Ratings would soar when she and gold medallist Misty May, of the women's Olympic beach volleyball team, verbally volleyed the weather report.

In the end, Shakespeare got it half right. A rose by any other name would smell as sweet, but if botanists had christened it "Spam," would we all want one in our garden?

Chapter Five: Almost Famous

The Quest for Success

Everybody wants to make a buck; some by conventional methods and others with flare. Either way, we all manage to scratch a little pocket change out of the dirt.

Luckily, Americans today still know how to create opportunity for themselves. They understand that the saying, "When my boat comes in . . .," refers to personally rowing it to shore and making something out of whatever they find when they get there.

And lean times lend themselves to desperate measures.

So I've got to applaud the ingenuity of a businessman, obviously thumbing his nose at animal rights activists, who advertises on his road-side sign, "For Sale, Corn and Orka." What I want to know is whether it's homegrown or imported from Sea World, filleted or chopped, fresh or frozen.

I also wonder if he's friends with the fellow advertising, on a similar handpainted board, "Peacock Meat."

Some folks just have the gift of persuasion and a handle on savvy sales techniques. The **Varity Store's** almost illegible hand written bill-board looked so unappealing, I pulled over to take a closer look. Peering through the dusty window, I hoped to catch a glimpse of a "varity." From what I could tell, "varities" might be old ladies, tube socks, stuffed animals, pots for catching leaks, or tacky lamps.

When it's not enough to generate inquisitiveness, however, a wise entrepreneur diversifies: "Guns, Live Bait & Bibles – If we don't have what you need, the Lord does." This particular place has a Yellow Pages listing under the heading, **Right Wing Christian Book Stores**.

Sometimes, the key to success lies in the appellation of an enterprise. Take **The Bank of Banks**, for instance, in, where else, but Banks County. That's a tough title to prove.

Or consider the **Quickie Restaurant** down in Albany, and its inspired menu offerings. I bet it's one of those places with walls full of autographed pictures of celebrities who have dined there. Bill Clinton's face, I suspect, smiles unapologetically at customers, along with those of philanderers, I mean fillet eaters, of all persuasions and politics.

Down the street from the Quickie, **Loosiers Furniture Mart** opens its doors each morning. The marquis doesn't indicate if the name refers to the proprietor or the customers, or both.

Crooks Automotive: What can I say? At least they're honest.

Other capitalists ensure profits by posting their expectations in plain view of the patron. No client of the **Pay-or-Go Trailer Park** ever claims confusion about the terms of the contract.

Of course, everyone in pursuit of financial reward needs a little nudge now and again. Barrie Dolnick left her senior VP position at a New York firm - knowing she would achieve far more as a voodoo doctor - to write her book, *Simple Spells for Success*. Now a creepy corporate consultant, she aids clients using tarot cards, astrology charts and incantations, while waving a magical chicken foot.

Her self-help manual even recommends a little black magic for people on the quest for success facing lean times: On a Friday in July, at 7pm, arrange a clump of weeds in a mason jar and light a citronella candle. Then, on your wife's heirloom tablecloth, place a pickled pig's foot with a silver dime between the toes. Toss some nuts (ones kin to you work best) around the room, and then sew up the table cloth with orange thread, knotting the ends sixty-thousand times.

Take three sips of wine. Then take 1,697 sips more. Things will seem better . . . until your wife discovers her tablecloth.

Or, you could get in on the ground floor of the Orka business.

The Lord Works in Mysterious Ways

The Lord works in mysterious ways . . . or life is cruel (take your pick).

Just ask the mother who blessed out the coach of her son's Little League team last spring, before storming off to the parking lot in a ruffled huff. She then exasperatedly dug through her purse in search of her keys, while her mortified children skulked about the perimeter of the car, doing their best to draw on the powers of invisibility.

When she had the entire contents of her purse emptied on the hood, one child, peering through the window, yelled, "Hey Mama, I see the keys!"

She, of course, had locked them in the car. And who, but the word-wounded coach, should happen along - the only person available to help the woman - with his very own coat hanger.

"Bring your dad with you next time kid," he advised with a wink of his eye and a cluck of his tongue. Then he holstered his hanger and rode off into the sunset in his pickup truck.

Ask the guy who sat to my right, and the girl who sat to my left, in Dr. Whitton's Chemistry 221 at the University of Georgia, during which the Teaching Assistant surreptitiously took roll on occasion. The day after the midpoint of the quarter came and went, taking with it the last opportunity to withdraw with a passing grade, the TA entered the lecture hall under Dr. Whitton's watchful gaze.

"As I call your name, please stand," he announced. When he reached the end of his list, half the class had risen for the occasion. "You may leave. You have been dropped with a failing grade from this course for missing more than five days."

The girl who sat to my left didn't make an appearance that day and continued coming to class (whenever she felt like it), taking exams, and completing labs. Her grade report, with a mark of WF, was her first sign that anything had gone awry.

Ask Arthur Gardner who attempted to break the Guinness Book record for marathon bowling. By the final hour, exhaustion claimed him, his back almost benched him, and his left ankle swelled over the top of his shoe like a water balloon under pressure.

But he exceeded the old record by four minutes.

While he, his family, and his fans celebrated this ridiculous fifteen minutes of distinction, a reporter arrived on the scene with the news that another fellow, also bonkers for bowling, had already broken, and reset, the record six weeks earlier. Gardner fell short of the new time by three hours and twenty-one minutes.

The reporter had fifty-five hours and twenty minutes to uncover the story of the unknown record-breaker. In addition, Gardner had a fifteen minute rest every eight hours. Had Gardner timed his celebration at the end of an eight hour stretch, and the reporter not arrived sixteen minutes too late, Gardner would have had the opportunity to continue bowling for his claim to fame.

And as for the guy who allegedly holds the current record, he became so delirious, during his own epic bowling adventure, that Guinness Book history will remember him as the sportsman who took to urinating down his own leg.

The next time you rent a pair of bowling shoes, I hope you will re-member that, yes, the Lord works in mysterious ways and life is cruel and you may just be wearing some record breaking shoes.

Daddy's Work Number

Blip-blip. *Blip-blip. Blip-blip.* [Official call center phone ringing.] "911 call center. State the nature of your emergency," requested the operator.

"May I speak with my daddy, please," asked a small child.

"Could you repeat what you said? I am uncertain that I heard you correctly. Is your daddy hurt or in some kind of trouble?"

"Yes, ma'am. No, ma'am. I'm not sure. May I speak to my daddy, Stan Willelp?"

"Honey, don't hang up."

Chonka-chonka-ooh-la-la, shazama-zam, loo-la. [Cell phone ringing.]

"Hello?"

"Is this Stan Willelp?"

"Yes."

"This is the McDuffie County 911 Emergency Response Call Center. Someone just placed a 911 call from your residence."

"No. No. No. That's not possible," insisted Stan. "No one is home at my house."

"We received a call from a female child. The computer identified the number as linked to your residence."

"I'm sorry. It can't be a call from my house. No one is home. My wife is right here with me and my children are next door with my mama."

"The young lady who called said she wanted to talk to her daddy. Could that be you?" The operator tried to maintain her composure.

"I'll call you back," said Stan.

Brrring. Brrring. Brrring. [Stan's mama's phone.]

"Hello?"

"Mama."

"Yeah. Still am. And, no, y'all can't come for dinner tonight. Other than that, whatcha need?"

"Mama, where's Leighann?"

"I sent her out to feed the chickens. She was bouncing off the walls in here with me. Last time I peeked out the kitchen window, I saw her in the yard playing."

"How long ago? Are you sure she's still out there?"

"Yep. Pretty sure. Why? What are you getting at," asked Mama, pulling back the curtains to get a better view of the back yard, irritated that her own son would doubt her ability to care for her grandchild.

"Someone is at our house calling 911."

Stan's Mama flinched from the sting. "Oh, Lordy. Let me call you back," she sighed, and hoofed it next door as fast as a granny can go.

Ta-ling-a-ling-a-ling. Ta-ling-a-ling-a-ling. Ta-ling-a-ling-a-ling. [Stans' home phone.] "Hello?" a familiar voice answered.

"Mama?" asked Stan, thinking he had dialed the wrong number. "What are you doing at my house? Are you the one calling 911?"

"NO! But I know who is," and a long, dangerous pause, like a bubble in an I.V. line, traveled from one receiver to the other. Stan listened hard to indistinct shuffling and whispering, attempting to decipher the mystery.

Finally a fragile, shaky, tearful voice said, "Daddy, I've been trying to call you!"

"Leighann," Stan scolded his daughter harshly, "you can only call 911 when there is an emergency."

"I know Daddy," she sniffled, unclear about her father's anger.

"So why did you call 911 asking to talk to me?"

"It's your work number," she plaintively explained.

"My work number? Whatever gave you that idea?!" exclaimed Stan.

"It's written on the side of the ambulance you drive. Just like the exterminator has his number on the side of the truck he drives."

"Um, hm." Stan let his daughter wade in the pool of silence gathering in the low place between them. Then he said, amused, "Have you been calling the exterminator, too?"

Double Dog Dare Ya!

Dod and Reba lived in Atlanta their entire married life; over thirty years. So when their last child finally moved out, so did Dod and Reba.

Dod retired from his law enforcement job of chasing cold-hearted criminals, and they started looking for land and a simpler life. Together, Reba and Dod sought serenity, fresh air, and friendly, but distant, neighbors. They wanted to get Dod the heck out of danger and get downright country fried.

In Rutledge, GA, they bought several acres with an old farmhouse and a long, meandering driveway. For the fun of it, they invested in a couple of cows, a few chickens, and a tractor. They didn't know how to use any of it, but liked the noises of rural living.

About 100 yards from the house, they planted a garden, and, from the wide front porch, spent the evenings watching their tomatoes ripen. Long conversations about politics, the kids, and the universe's purpose for bovine took place over the din of chirping crickets.

Many a glass of wine accompanied their postulations.

One late-summer evening, sometime in September, Dod and Reba retreated to the veranda to share a fine Vognier. After his initial glass, feeling high on the cool night air, Dod got a little giddy and challenged Reba, "I bet you're too chicken to strip your clothes and run touch the garden gate."

Reba waved him off with her hand.

Dod poured them each another glassful, which they sipped, enjoying the sensation of summer stepping aside for fall. Several minutes passed and Dod, feeling his luck improved now, again threw out the dare.

"Underwear and everything," asked Reba. She enjoyed watching him squirm with excitement over the perceived possibility.

"Yep," said Dod. "I dare ya to do it."

"You know I won't do any such thing," Reba scolded. Secretly, however, she felt delighted that he still wanted to see her birthday suit.

"Brock-bock-bock," Dod imitated a cackling hen.

Topping off their glasses with the last of the evening fare, Reba bristled. "Dod, I'm a fifty-six year-old woman and I can do anything I darn well please, and if I want to run to the garden stark naked, I will. But you can't make me."

"Because you won't," goaded Dod.

"Will too, when I'm good and ready," she snapped.

"Double dog dare ya."

Reba downed the elixir of courage, stood, and unbuttoned her blouse.

A surprised, but pleased, Dod, sealed the deal. "Nahhh, Reba, I know you. I'm not that easy." He exposed a smile so big his dangling uvula showed and rocked back in his chair, satisfied that she wouldn't back down now.

Reba tossed her blouse onto the porch rail and unsnapped her shorts. Her foundation garments followed. She stood before Dod in her full God-given glory. "Watch this," she said.

Reba jogged to the garden fence and bent over to catch her breath. About that time, the sound of car tires on the cattle gate echoed down the driveway. Reba's ears pricked. Her legs felt like noodles.

Dod yelled, "Whoo, Reba, you better run, girl. Sounds like we got company." Dod stared down the driveway, like he could see a trail of dust winding toward his homestead. Really, he saw a truck pull in and back out.

Reba sprinted toward the house, her flesh moving in motions contra-dictory to her feet.

When she had twenty-five yards to go, he scooped up her clothes and scooted inside.

"I'm a chicken now, Dod," she screamed. "I'm a wet hen!"

Dod quaked with laughter at the noises of rural living.

Mama Always Told You So

The news poured in that Viagra, and other "recreational" drugs like it, has side effects, other than the obvious, allegedly causing sudden blindness in 43 satisfied customers. The reported cases of ocular lights-out occurred within hours of ingesting the mood enhancing medicine.

Now the FDA plans to develop new labeling requirements for uppers of this kind. I have a few re-labeling suggestions of my own:

> 1) **CAUTION:** If you purchased this product from those crazy Canadians across the northern border, who sell pharmaceuticals at unheard of low prices here in the states, then many politicians would have you believe it may be tainted. Canadians secretly conspire to take over North America, and they will do it by blinding one randy old goat at a time.

> 2) **WARNING:** Old men may go blind, before or after taking this medication; in both cases probably due to a stroke. Nevertheless, those fortunate few who lose their sight subsequent to taking advantage of some pretty octogenarian, or, rather, some prescribed pills, may have grounds for a law suit.

> 3) **NOTICE:** Your mother always told you if you diddled with it too much, the Lord would strike you blind. So far God has gone easy on you by only taking away your potency. Forty-three done-got-lucky sots, however, who didn't heed His warning, are now sightless. Use at your own risk.

Men report they will continue to take the gamble for a night of unbridled passion, particularly since many users find themselves nearing the end of the life cycle and desire to go out on top. They still believe it's a good bang for their buck and, not only that, they also quite enjoy groping in the dark.

Nick Ransom of Atlanta summed it up nicely for an AJC reporter when he said, "Given the nature of the product and what it does, you have to remember that men have risked far more than their eyes."

Mr. Ransom shared his insight, and added to his credibility, while teasing death itself to meet a mate. He chanced bodily obliteration beneath a fully functioning, erect, twenty-five story crane, high above Peachtree Road, from which another desperate fellow taunted the sensibilities of citizens, and ran the possibility of plummeting onto voyeurs below.

Apparently, the crowd of spectators gawking at the stand-off included hot chicks. I suppose Mr. Ransom hoped, just by looking so brave in the face of danger, some of the high emotion might get directed toward him.

So really, the men grow older but their methods and motivations generally remain the same, with a little tweaking by the folks at Pfizer. The one difference between young guys and old guys is the lines they use to coerce sweet things into yielding to their affections.

Young chaps commonly bank on the persuasive powers of, "If you love me, you will." And although many of us can think of other claims lads have made about undue physical harm, only Dr. Ruth Westheimer could get away with mentioning them here.

Old dudes, however, for the moment, may have more pull than the whippersnappers; when they say "C'mon honey. I've got less than four hours left on this meter, and if you don't, I might go blind," they actually, now, have a small amount of evidence to back it up. And, knowing seventy-five year-olds, they can probably whip out an AARP sponsored medical report in the heat of the moment.

But you old gals need to be savvier than your teenage counterparts, and say, "Well, then, honey, I guess that you won't Cialis anymore."

Strategic Errors

Once upon a time, in the Kingdom of Anythinkinappen, a prince of a man, named Anyjoe, went off to college to seek his fortune. He studied very, very hard and earned a degree in photography. But, as in all fairy tales, somebody wicked convinced him he had no gift for taking pictures of flowers from odd angles.

Consequently, Prince Anyjoe, downhearted, aimlessly drove his worthy steed across the countryside, ending up at an army recruiting office. He joined, hoping to fulfill his royal destiny.

At basic training, while in drill formation, Anyjoe's sergeant called him forward. "Sir, yes sir!" shouted the recruit, wanting to survive this encounter with as few push-ups as possible.

"What instrument do you play, plebe?"

"Instrument, sir?"

"Don't mock me boy. Drop and do fifty."

After counting out his punishment, the lad regained his feet and took his place in line.

"I didn't tell you to step back in line," the officer gruffly coughed. "What instrument do you play?"

"Sir, I don't play an instrument, sir," Anyjoe replied, feeling confused.

The sergeant stomped heavily toward Anyjoe, until they stood nose to nose. "Don't play games with me boy," he barked, sending spittle onto his prey. "You would rather have your fellow swine here think you're a band geek than have me up your hindquarters for the duration."

"Sir, yes sir!"

Later that day, after running twenty-five miles (five extra for insubordination), he visited, as directed, the major general's office. "Sit down, son. We seem to have a little problem. You didn't indicate on your application which instrument you play." Then the major general leaned forward and took on a menacing timbre, "You know, it's a violation of military policy, worthy of court marshal, to lie to a commanding officer."

"Yes, sir. I don't play an instrument, sir. I don't understand why everyone keeps asking me, sir."

Continuing, the major general held up official papers. "I have the results of your army aptitude test. You scored off the charts, genius level, on musical ability. How do you explain that?"

"I can't, sir." Prince Anyjoe now feared an accusation of cheating. But something even worse happened.

For the next four years he peeled potatoes and pulled KP. On his leave time, however, Anyjoe studied the saxophone. Due to his government issued musical acuity, he learned rapidly and soon mastered the sax, beyond his instructor's wildest expectations.

Anyjoe became an adult prodigy, surpassing the skills of jealous royal minstrels, who spent their whole lives studying music to develop barely equal expertise. Soon, he jammed with a jazz band that could swing like the queen's meow and got gigs all over the kingdom.

Upon discharge, he met with the major general for an exit interview. "Have a seat son. I have the obligation to ask if you'd like to re-enlist. It's a good life with excellent benefits. If you stay on, I could see about advancing your rank. Perhaps you could supervise the potato peelers."

"Thank you, sir. The army has been good for me. I found myself here."

"Ahh, yes. We do have a way of molding people into being all they can be."

"Yes, sir," Anyjoe said. "And I'm going to be a professional sax player."

"Uh, yeah. About that music thing. I'm also charged with telling you that an audit revealed your test results were flawed. In fact, you have no propensity for music whatsoever. Son, you have an uncanny talent for photographing flowers at peculiar angles."

Prince Anyjoe left the army and played his sax happily ever after in the Kingdom of Mindovermatter.

ext.

The Slippery Underslide

Every spring, as the days butt up against summer, my husband, in the party rentals business, brings home his 15-foot tall waterslide for a weekend.

Last year, on a Sunday afternoon, while our children clung to the final fistful of fun, a rickety, blue truck pulled alongside the curb. Not an unusual occurrence, since we live in a small town. Many people stop and roll down their windows to ask where we got the slide, gawk at the mayhem, or needle bystanding adults to get wet.

So when my husband and I saw a man, a woman, and two children clamber out of the cab, we didn't think much of it; just that they were bolder than the rest. The woman marched up to the front porch, while the man trailed behind. The children stood in the wet grass.

"Do you know these people," I whispered to my husband.

"Never seen them before," he mumbled.

"Hey, y'all," the woman greeted us. "That yore waterslide?"

My husband gave a quick advertisement.

"Mmmm," she vocalized. "This here's my boyfriend, Olin. We been drivin' by a few times and seen you out here. My kids sure would like to try it." Olin stood nearby with his hands in his jeans pockets, nodding in support, but never making eye contact with us.

While I thought, *Not just bold, but audacious,* my easy going other half said, "Let them take their shoes off and have a turn."

At that she turned and screeched, "Okay! Take yer shoes off. You better mind, too." The kids, a boy about nine and a girl about seven, tore around to the ladder, thrilled at their remarkable fortune.

"Alright," she said, "we'll be back in 'bout a hour. Y'all don't know how much this means to them. Come on, Olin." Olin followed her, giddy about the clever offload. Before we could process or protest, they climbed into the creaky, old truck and eased off.

I looked at my husband, who returned my perplexed expression. Neither of us said anything. We stared at the two children we had accidentally acquired. We didn't even know their names, much less if they were prone to seizures or allergic reactions.

My spouse speculated, "I wonder what our liability is on this?"

I had bigger questions. "I wonder what made them think it's okay to drop their children off with total strangers? I wonder where they're going? I wonder who we call in case of an emergency?"

I took a breath, but couldn't quit. "I wonder how that conversation went? - 'Those people look safe. Think their dog bites? You kids play at that house while Olin and me go take care of some business.' - I wonder if those people are ever coming back?!!!!"

An hour and a half later, long after my children had gone inside for baths, our visitors remained. "What do we do with them?" I muttered to my husband.

About that time, the tired truck lumbered down the street. Olin sat behind the wheel grinning like a bullfrog. The woman stepped out and hollered, "Y'all come on now and let these folks take that thang down." The children glumly shuffled toward the truck, scooping up their shoes and socks.

I felt so relieved to see Olin, I could have hugged his neck. Except he looked like he'd already had it hugged.

Again, the woman yelled, "Git yerselves up to that porch and tell them people thank you!" Olin nodded.

Moments later, they drove off. My husband and I silently exchanged our same dumbfounded gazes and closed the door behind us.

Killing Crows

Man's ingenuity never ceases to amaze me. For example, I recently learned that one way to manage human waste involves recycling it as fertilizer. Once reformulated, planes fly it over tree farms and do a dump.

I commend the civil engineer who devised this plan, and I thank my realtor, particularly on windy days, for not locating me near key targets.

One of the side effects of this process, besides the obvious, is that it attracts flocks of scavenger birds from all corners of the county. Maybe the smell lures them. Maybe they find it food worthy. At any rate, so many come that they begin roosting in neighborhoods, greatly alarming residents with small children.

How does one combat carnivorous collectors of carrion?

One friend casually mentioned the difficulty to a team of sharp shooters. Well, okay, really just a guy, with a couple of 16 gauge shotguns, and his eight year old daughter. The following week, armed, and slightly dangerous, they stalked through her backyard seeking a quick kill.

Blam! Blam!

Blam, blam, blam!

Nothing hit the ground but a squirrel caught in the crossfire.

The birds loped a little higher in the trees and looked at the pair with curiosity, while salivating over the rodent.

Quickly, the child's father designed a plan. He displayed her on the ground in the open part of the yard, and instructed her in how to take on the shroud of rigor mortis. Then he crept into the cover of the azaleas, where he patiently waited for the buzzards to begin circling.

"Hold on, honey," he whispered loudly. "I think they've spotted you. Yep, they're starting to spiral. Be brave."

Still suspicious, however, the feathered foragers hung high on the air currents, out of range of the exterminators.

Seeing the apprehension of the prey, the courageous hunter hit upon an even better idea. Why not place the deceased squirrel on the chest of the young girl, to create an even more enticing smorgasbord?

And so, there lay the young thespian, doing her best impression of three-day-old road kill with a cherry on top.

Suddenly, the vultures developed an interest in the table spread and descended with great velocity. "Here they come, baby," shouted the dad. "Don't move until you see their beaks near your eyes." He trembled with excitement.

Well, about this time, my friend drove into her driveway. Getting out of her vehicle, she heard gunshots from her backyard and saw a figure doing a belly crawl through her pine island.

She hit the ground, until the fellow jumped up and identified himself. But before she recovered sufficiently to inquire into his intentions, his kid rounded the corner of the house at a quick clip, glancing behind herself, clutching the departed squirrel.

"Daddy, they got too close. I thought they would peck my eyes out," she said, as sort of an apology for leaving her live-bait post.

"How would a fur ball peck your eyes out? And why are you hunting it in my backyard?" My friend shook her head in exasperation.

They explained that the child used the dead animal to charm the buzzards.

"I don't think you want birds like that eating out of your hands," my pal advised.

"Oh, no ma'am. She played possum with it." He seemed a little confused, like he didn't understand why my friend wouldn't want him making bunkers with her crossties.

In the end, despite aggravation over attempted avian annihilation in her backyard, she reflected favorably on the advantages of living in a small town, where mere mention of a need motivates neighbors indeed.

Chapter Six

Variations on a Variorium

Mr. Willie, the church custodian, went to town to get an MRI. The nurse went through her routine questions necessary before sliding him into the magnetic tube. At last she asked, "Are you claustrophobic, Mr. Willie?"

"Oh naw, ma'am," he said. "I ain't at'al afraid of heights."

You've Got Mail

You've got mail.

SCROLL.
Hoper@byrandis.org.
Subject: Re: Cub Scout camp.

Hoper? Cub Scout camp?

OPEN.
Hey Danille! Cute Pictures! You are very active with your son. That's wonderful.

Wait a minute. I'm not Danille. I have a friend named Danille, who sent me pictures of her son who is in cub scouts. Odd.

I just bought a digital camera. I would like to e-mail pictures to people but I can't figure out how to do it. I'm trying to help a friend send some pictures for his work. If your sending a bunch of pictures, do you have to make a folder first and then send them like that? Help.

Shouldn't that be y-o-u-'-r-e instead of y-o-u-r? Why am I reading this?

I'm going to teach Kindergarten next year. I'm a little nervous about that. I've been teaching 1st for three years and 4th before that.

They're going to demote her right on down to the daycare diaper room if she doesn't straighten out the you're/your problem. Good heavens, I'm awful.

I'm seeing this guy named Gordon. He's very handsome and very sweet. He's a bit of a flirt with everyone, however. I've been off and on seeing him for the past three years. This time it's been more frequently that I see him. Or, should I say, he's living with me.

Well that's quite a segue to a confession. Ugh. This really is none of my business. That's pretty often that she's seeing him, though. Doesn't sound like he has his head in the same game she does. I should close this.

I'm not sure how long he's going to be staying here. It's been so great, now I don't want him to go. Anyhow, a little sisterly advice?

Don't hit **REPLY ALL** when sharing personal information over the Internet.

Did you ever live with your husband?

For better and for worse, for the past 17 years.

I figure it's a good way to see how people really are. Write back. Cantella.

What should I do? What should I do? She didn't ask *me* specifically. Someone needs to tell her that everyone in Danille's address book just read of Cantella's live-in relationship. No. How mortifying for her. Close this. Do it. Click the red X.

REPLY.
Dear Cantella, You accidentally replied to ALL. I feel like a terrible eavesdropper. Sorry. Tried to stop myself several times, but I admittedly have no self-control. I do, however, have the advice you asked for. First of all, the contraction for you are is spelled y-o-u-'-r-e not y-o-u-r.
Secondly, may I suggest that you read the instructions for your digital camera. Or better yet, have Gordon read them and e-mail his own pictures for work.

Which brings me to something very important. DON'T LIVE WITH GORDON. He won't leave until you bring up the nasty M-word. Why would he? He gets what he wants whenever he wants it. Plus meals, housekeeping, and laundry service. And why would you want to see what a man is like before you marry him? That's the craziest thing I ever heard! My incredibly wonderful husband has this annoying habit of neatly folding his dirty socks like they're (contraction for they are) clean. He eats fried livers. He makes smacking noises in his sleep. Had I known about all this prior to saying I-do, I may not have wed him.

I apologize for intruding. Since we are both school teachers, I will put my final thoughts in those terms: Don't write with crayons and then get upset that you can't erase your mistakes.

Danille's friend, Lucy
SEND.

Buzzard Off!

ALERT! ALERT! Sound the sirens! Vultures have invaded nearby Warrenton! Heard it on the radio, read it in the paper, that piles of pigeon droppings are accumulating at rapid rates. What they've got, by all accounts, is a nesting population of Turkey Vultures; what some folks call Turkey Buzzards. Committees have convened to determine just what to do about this menace that moved into those once quiet and well-kept neighborhoods. Specialists have been called in to trouble-shoot.

Meanwhile, city workers have decided to hang dead - from natural causes - buzzards in the trees where the vultures congregate so as to make them evacuate. These ugly birds are protected under the International Migratory Bird Treaty. Therefore, the Department of Natural Resources may assist by helping city workers fill out special applications for licenses to shoot live turkey buzzards, which will supply even more dead bodies to hang from tree limbs.

An esteemed ornithologist indicated that the feathery friends obviously stay because the fair city offers a fine source of food; for turkey buzzards that would be carrion. That's all they eat; nothing more. Not even small children as I first feared. Thus, city employees have run reconnaissance missions to locate and eliminate the food source, to no avail.

Well, look up! Look up! There's dead, decomposing, delicious, aromatic meat hanging in the trees. Those birds have practically been fed on silver platters, served breakfast, lunch, and dinner in bed. We may as well give them turndown service with chocolates on their pillows. Every vulture from the highway to the high school has called his brother Phil in Mizzoula and told him to bring the family out for spring break.

So, I've got some other research-based suggestions for eradication:

1) Shake the trees after the vultures have settled into their roost at dusk. Caution: Wear a raincoat. Vultures will defend themselves by puking a putrid rain of vomit upon their attackers.

2) Make noise by frequently running outside, clapping and shouting (the mayor could lead city council members in this), or setting off firecrackers throughout the week (any random boy will oblige).

3) Hang shiny, fluttery objects in the roost. Since a small town operates on a tight budget, municipal employees could just brush metallic paint on the corpses they've already hung. (Careful. This can backfire. Vultures are curious and playful. They may discover that the objects pose no risk, at which point shiny stuff will instead become fun toys. When combined

with the scent of decay, these toys may actually lure more birds.)

4) Squirt high-powered jets of water by aiming an ordinary sprinkler head into the trees. According to watering restrictions, vultures on the even side of the street can be discouraged on Monday, Wednesday, and Friday. Vultures on the odd side of the street can be deterred on Tuesday, Thursday, and Saturday.

5) Periodic cannon blasts have been known to work, but are almost as equally disconcerting as the vermin themselves.

If the mayor refuses to run through the streets clapping and yelling every evening, may I propose adoption? Post it on the city website that people can adopt a vulture for a nominal fee, a portion of which will cover whitewash cleanup. For $50, the adoptive parent will receive naming rights for his buzzard, an adoption certificate, a framed photo, weekly e-mail reports on the avian's activities, and a secret Webkinz code.

Turn off the sirens and put up the Webkinz link, so adoptive parents can begin caring for and playing with their Buzzardkins right away.

Chain Mail

O n January 4, my husband received the following letter:

> *Dear Mr. Adams,*
>
> *Knowing that you are a compassionate businessman, I want to inform you of a terminally ill boy's dying wish.*
>
> *Craig Chergold is a 7 year-old who has brain cancer. His ambition is to enter the Guinness Book of World Records for owning the largest collection of business cards. Please send your card to the Make a Wish Foundation.*
>
> *In addition, recopy this request onto your letterhead and forward it to 10 companies in your area.*
>
> *Through this small effort, you and I can make a big difference.*
> *Sincerely,*
> *Shirley Allgood*
> *Acme, Inc.*

On January 5th, my spouse, a kindhearted man, who also loves to receive anything other than invoices in the mail, asked one of his employees to retype the plea and send one copy to each of the 10 local businesses on the list he compiled.

"Uhm, Mr. Adams, what is this for," she inquired.

"A little boy who has cancer and may die. We need to help him," he replied.

"Yes, sir. The letters will go out today. Why don't we send twenty?"

"Okay, go for it," he enthusiastically encouraged.

On February 20th, a similar letter arrived in the Monday mailbag:

> *Dear Mr. Adams,*
>
> *Greg Sherhold is a 17 year-old boy with terminal cancer. His greatest desire is to be listed in the Guinness Book as the person who collected the largest number of business cards. To give continuity to this action, please send your card to the Make a Wish Foundation, and pass this request on to as many people as possible.*
>
> *Time is short for Greg, so respond quickly.*
> *Yours Truly,*
> *Ken U. Elp*
> *Widget Workers United*

"It looks like a race to see who can get in the Guinness Book first," mused my beloved.

He instructed the same employee to retype the request and make copies, saying, "We need to help this kid, too, but I secretly hope the seven year-old wins. Either way, how exciting for these guys. It gives them something to smile about."

"Yeah. What was that other kid's name?"

"I can't remember."

On March 14, a fellow Chamber member penned a response:

Dear Mr. Adams,

Do not send anymore dying kids' petitions for business cards. You are the victim of a hoax. We can't believe you've never seen this one. This chain letter has gone around the World Wide Web so many times it quit aging.

The family of this child and the Make a Wish Foundation don't want all those stupid cards. It's a recycling and postal nightmare.

Get a life. Get on the Internet.

Fondly,
Sao R. Grips
Nohitall Farms

Further research revealed that in 1989 a nine year-old kid named Craig Shergold really did have a brain tumor. Relatives waged a greeting card campaign to get him into the Guinness Book. In 1991, a philanthropist paid for surgery to remove the tumor. Oddly, over 200 million business cards have been sent to him. Today, Craig Shergold is a healthy twenty-eight year-old who only wants business cards with his own name printed on them.

He doesn't need his own card, however, he needs me. We'll both get rich. I'll put him, "The man urban legends are made of," on the speakers' circuit. We'll write his biography, *As the Chain Mail Churns*, and compose a book for dummies, advising the minions on how they, too, can become the heroes of modern myths. Together, we'll do book tours and freak shows.

Does anyone have Mr. Shergold's address, so I can send him my business card?

Variations on a Variorium

"**A**variorium? What the heck is a variorium," I asked, reading it aloud from the newspaper to my confounded cat. Scattering column drafts and a feline around my desk, I searched for the dictionary, in vain. So, to avoid killing my unnerved cat with curiosity, I took my need for knowledge to the streets. Much to my surprise, I'm the only person in the southeast who doesn't have some handle on the gist of "variorium."

Dr. Glenilda Miller, principal at Mithrosa Elementary in Mithrosa, Mississppi says, "Oh yes, a variorium. We hold one each spring in the cafetorium. Parents, students, and teachers all enter hoping to win the grand prize of a trip to the sanatorium."

Just as confidently, Bubba McCree of Blountville, Alabama tells me he caught a "biggun" out of Mudshank Lake with a red wiggler and a piece of corn. "Gawl darnit," he exclaimed, "if it ain't the biggest variorium on record in the whole dern state."

But a spirited young lady sitting next to me on the Milledge bus during my recent spin around the University of Georgia campus in Athens assures me that, as a music major, she knows a variorium when she hears one. Her favorite is Bach's seventh in A minor. She whistled a few notes, before getting off at the Beta-don't-know-an-Iota house, and I had to agree that it's certainly a lovely score.

Elmsdale Gregory Frumpton, III, of Columbia, South Carolina, concurs that the word pertains to music. He relates that he recently attended a symphony concert in which the first and second varioriums performed a duet.

On the other hand, my favorite college professor, Dr. Tokalot, who gives brown bag lunch presentations on the third Friday of each month in Heerhim Hall, discussed the planetary and solunar evolution of varioriums, back in October.

A fifth grader at Blockwood Academy, a private educational institution in Zebulon, North Carolina responds, "Variorium, v-a-r. Can you use it in a sentence, please?"

Barrett Goshen of Nagel, Kentucky tried to trade in his Pinto for a Variorium, but didn't have enough cash or credit. He bought a Chevette instead.

Dixie Ann Parton of Sevierville, Tennessee, who boasts status as a fourth cousin, two times removed, of Miss Dolly herself, warns me that, "They're mean little critters; worse than a wanton wharf rat in heat."

Buster Buchannon, a gardener in Howsendown, Virginia, feels certain that it's a nearly extinct variety of orchid. He is single handedly attempting to reintroduce it to the tropics of Havana. I saw some growing in his greenhouse with my very own eyes. Funny, none of the large, leafy plants he showed me looked much like orchids.

And Leslie Jack, my cousin-in-law from Aintevergetinout, Arkansas, vaguely remembers having a mixed drink called a Flaming Variorium. She says as she recalls she liked it, "But it burned like a mother going down." I tried to get the recipe, but she passed out.

My dear friend Luleen Wallerstein thanked me for reminding her to get her prescription refilled.

Finally, my children insist it's a good name for a pet. How would you like to holler Variorium while kicking the cat?

It tweaks me.

Alas, however, an errant key stroke is the elusive root origin of this graceful, lilting compilation of letters. A type-o! I searched the world over to find meaning in a type-o!

The intended word was, in fact, variorum. And this story, by a small stretch, and a leap, happens to be one; one of the best in the whole dern state, if I do say so myself.

The Leaning Tower of Pisa

Last week I received this e-mail:

> I continue to enjoy your column. I read it in the Tennessee Star Journal.
> Your recent Happy New Year was not only humorous but your words, "I
> will not say 'no' simply because I'm afraid of what will happen if I say
> 'yes'"...were useful, life enriching advice . . . Thanks for all you do, Walt.

Walt's note triggered the nerd nodule on my DNA and spurred me to
think about the Leaning Tower of Pisa.

Construction on the Leaning Tower of Pisa, originally planned as a
vertical edifice - the bell tower for the city's cathedral - began in 1173. Designed by architect Bonanno Pisano, the tower, by the end of the first five
years of construction, noticeably leaned to the south. Progress halted with
only three stories completed.

I picture, and empathize with, Pisano, distressed, gazing at the aber-
ration of his blueprint, ruminating over why he ever said "Yes" to the
project that sagged with certain failure, tortured by the revelation, not to
mention the monument-sized public display, of his inadequacies. Still,
although he and his team quit, they did not give up. They did not raze the
eyesore. They merely walked away in consternation, pausing to ponder a
solution to the problem.

Almost one hundred years passed as artisans considered the angled
campanile. In 1272, new brains, fresh hands, set to work again, first attempting to bolster the foundation. Just as it had Pisano, disappointment
beset this group determined to right a wrong. Yet, instead of throwing
their hands in the air and cursing Pisano's name, they soldiered on.

The team added four more floors, gradually building straight up from
the lower stories, hoping, one might suppose, to apply an opposing force.
In reality, however, they created an ironic salute to the tower's original
visionary. Their efforts resulted in an obvious banana curve in the construction, which would also result in a banana curve in how history re-
membered Bonanno Pisano.

As the tower continued to increasingly list, progress again ceased. No
doubt, the latest craftsmen, like those before them, spent days and weeks,
even months, reviewing their plans and recalculating the math, trying to
pinpoint their errors, questioning why they said "Yes," when they should
have shouted, "No, no, no," and run from it like they would a skunk in

heat.

Another century passed. In 1372, the bell chamber atop the threatening-to-tumble tower was assembled. For the first time in years, the slant slowed, and, for a while, in the centuries following, even ended. Over time, people came to believe the builders of the Torre Pendente intended for it to lean.

Later, during World War II, American forces, threatened by snipers, were ordered to destroy all the towers in the city of Pisa. With only one remaining, the Leaning Tower, they received a last minute order to retreat. Miraculously, despite the strange structure's constant threat to destroy itself, it alone was spared.

Pisano, and those who worked to finish what he started, would be stunned that not only is the Leaning Tower of Pisa still precariously leaning, but that it is also one of the world's greatest wonders, mystifyingly defying gravity. This architectural blunder, seemingly at its tipping point, yet strong enough to survive wars, weather, and time, proves that our biggest failures can become our biggest successes, depending on how we tilt them. Therefore, I renew my vow to never say, "No," simply because I'm afraid of what will happen if I say, "Yes." Imagine the banana curves that'll throw into things.

Thanks for the reminder, Walt.

Bad Luck: The Real Thing

It's bad luck to start a fire in your fireplace or wood stove in May. That's what folks at the local feed store say. Start a fire in May and the hay won't grow, they say. I can only guess how they came to say it:

One day Ned said to Jubral, "Jubral?"

"Yeah, Ned."

"I wonder why our hay won't grow?"

"I don't know, Ned. Did we do anythin' outin the ordinary this year?"

"Well let me think, Jubral. You know, we had a chilly spring. Remember that fire we lit to keep warm one mornin'?"

"Yep."

"I reckon that's why our hay won't grow, Ned."

"I bet yer right, Jubral. No more fires in May."

I'm rather skeptical. Weird coincidence I'll give you, but bad luck? The hay field actually catching on fire from a spark a-fly from the wood-stove is bad luck. And that's just my point. Bad luck strikes swift and sure and in your face. Folks don't have to do a whole lotta thinkin' to figure it out.

In fact, I can name quite a few things that genuinely qualify as bad luck.

Taking your kids to adopt a plump, healthy male cat from the animal shelter and waking up two weeks later to find five baby kittens in your underwear drawer is bad luck. Getting a beautiful butterfly tattoo on the small of your back when you're seventeen, only to turn around at age 40 to discover a hideous moth crawling down your backside is bad luck.

Going on summer vacation and returning home to find that your house has been invaded by bats is bad luck. A dead bat in the guest bathroom, undetected by you, but promptly noted by the noses of your guests, is bad luck.

One brother throwing the other brother's t-shirt in the toilet of a port-o-let is bad luck. Your child asking you to retrieve his t-shirt from the toilet of a port-o-let is worse luck.

The roof leaking, again - bad luck.

Termites - bad luck.

Losing a contact lens in the shower - bad luck.

Someone throwing a baseball at your face while he shouts, "Think fast," and you don't, is bad luck.

Running over your white dog basking in the sun, camouflaged on your white concrete driveway, is bad luck.

Milk going sour before the expiration date is bad luck.

Cracking open a hardboiled, pink Easter egg to find yourself about to take a big bite of a partially gestated, boiled baby chick is bad luck.

Your parents making pork chops out of your overgrown pet pig, or fried chicken from your AWOL rabbit, Sir Hare, is bad luck.

Eating bad sushi - bad luck.

The washing machine getting off balance and shaking so hard that it goes through the floor - bad luck.

Your kids filling the air vents in the rental car with quarters - bad luck. Getting your finger stuck in the vent because you're trying to dig them out to pay at a toll booth - bad luck.

Dropping your cell phone in the neighbor's toilet is bad luck.

Your wife saying, "Honey, I'm pregnant, again," is bad luck.

Your arch social nemesis wearing the same outfit as you to a prime social gathering is bad luck.

Therefore, fires in May and the price of tea in China have nothing to do with omens of ill fortune. And I feel most certain that letting Ned and Jubral figure out crop fluctuations is surefire shootin' bad luck.

Don't Sell Chickens to the Voodoo Lady

Disclaimer: May 4th is International Respect for Chickens Day. Even though this story kills two birds with one stone, no chickens were hurt in the process.

Being southern and all, I'm a bit obsessive about rules. Only I like to refer to them, properly, as etiquette. Folks need such things. Otherwise we'd run around hilly-nilly, like chickens (no offense to the poultry) with our heads cut off, bumping into each other wearing white shoes after Labor Day and forgetting to say, "Excuse me, ma'am."

Before I round the curve of logic and forget what I needed to say in the first place, let me get back to business - the business of yard sales, garage sales, moving sales, and the general getting-rid-of-junk-that-has-piled-up-since-my-Aunt-Nita-decided-the-best-way-to-avoid-a-relapse-into-destitution-after-the-Great-Depression-was-to-horde-Styrofoam-meat-trays-in-her-attic sales - because I wish to save chickens.

These Saturday morning forays into fodder, however, require a certain elegance, grace, and precise understanding of the nuances of negotiation; in short, protocol. (Lest you fear I've taken leave of my senses, I will return to the chickens in due time.)

First of all, never try to give a sofa away for free. Some customers' hackles rise in response to grossly offensive charity. Other potential patrons, at hearing of the couch's pricelessness, will sniff it suspiciously and ask for an oral historical account, or recoil from it as if a Great Dane had given birth to eight puppies on it the day before. They all will depart empty handed.

Even if it's worthless, put a five buck price tag on the couch to keep from hauling it off yourself. "Five dollars! What a deal," people will exclaim, all clamoring to make the payoff and load it in their trucks.

Secondly, when someone offers to buy all twenty-seven faded, threadbare, mothball scented, cotton-polyester blend, mismatched pillowcases for $3.00, sell them. Do not say, "Well, I don't know. At the store they would cost a lot more than that."

It's a yard sale, not Walmart. Inexplicably, the purchaser wants to take a greasy-headed, exhausted-looking stranger's used linens home. Garage sale hosts really have no negotiating power. Accept this.

Third, all sales should be confidential; particularly when a nine year-old boy buys two quarter-sticks of dynamite, a rusty pocket knife, and a roll of fire crackers. Give the kid a break. The three quarters, seven dimes and two nickels burned a bigger hole in his pocket than some old humidified explosives will.

Fourth, yard sale shoppers should refrain from picking up items from a neighbor – wigs, skirts, black trench coats, partially used containers of fertilizer - that might generate suspicion. Just stand around fondling those items with your eyeballs, thinking dubious thoughts about the neighbor.

Fifth, buying a coffee maker for one dollar that may or may not work is a worthy risk. Savor the thrill of the anticipation while waiting for it to drip. If it doesn't function, don't go marching back over to return it. Put it in your garage.

Finally, when the voodoo lady shows up, wallet bulging, speaking freely of hexes and vexes and folks she has laid to waste one way or another, avoid eye contact. Resist the temptation of exchanging measly, dented muffin pans for dolls of thine enemies, with all the stick pin accessories included. If she wants the free couch after the mark up, give it to her and help her load it.

But, and this is very important in terms of respecting certain breeds of fowl, and it will require moral resoluteness on your part, whatever happens, however much she offers you, don't sell any of your chickens to the voodoo lady.

Wordly Wise, Wordly Woes

In a recent on-line article on leadership, the author wielded words like Xerox subsidy, adminisphere, and salmon day. Another piece on American culture included acronyms, WOOF, SMUM, DINK, without explanation, as if any random idiot would recognize them.

I consulted my Webster. Unfortunately, even though he used to know it all, he doesn't have a clue anymore.

Are you wordly wise, or do you, like me, suffer wordly woes. Take my test on modern vocabulary to find out:

1. Ringxiety (n.):
   a. An intense and uncontrollable fear of commitment.
   b. A phobia of bells.
   c. An ailment common among circus performers.
   d. In a crowd, trepidation over not knowing whose cell phone rang.

2. Cryovacking (v.):
   a. Removing crying youngsters from a crowded restaurant.
   b. Vacuuming in cold weather.
   c. Preserving dead bodies for future animation by vacuum-pack ing and then freezing them.
   d. Cooking vacuum-packed food by slowly warming it in water.

3. Guyliner (n.):
   a. Phrases single women say to meet men.
   b. Phrases single men say to meet women.
   c. Phrases single men say to meet men.
   d. Eyeliner designed for and used by men.

4. Cankles (n.):
   a. Mouth sores.
   b. The obstetrical term for the sounds newborn babies make.
   c. A type of candy similar to skittles.
   d. Another name for tree-trunk legs.

5. Face-blind (n.):
   a. The piece of fabric that covers the face of Muslim women.
   b. A roll down brim on a hat, designed to block the sun.
   c. A strategy for boxing-out opponent players in soccer.
   d. An inability to recognize faces.

6. Banana fold (n.):
    a. An origami technique.
    b. The place on the banana peel where it laps over itself when loosened from the fruit.
    c. A banana tree farm and all the people living there.
    d. Excess fat below the butt.

7. Feature fatigue (n.):
    a. A condition suffered by beauty pageant contestants.
    b. What happens to hot, prime-time television shows after running several seasons.
    c. The proper diagnosis, required by insurance companies, to justify the medical necessity of plastic surgery.
    d. Mental exhaustion caused by products that come with too many functions and buttons.

8. Dirt pill (n.):
    a. What a person takes when getting a dose of her own medicine.
    b. A new, suburban housewife way of condensing gossip for easier dissemination.
    c. The latest trend in birthday-party treats for preschoolers.
    d. A pill designed to stimulate the immune systems of children with allergies.

9. Muffin top (n.):
    a. A Dorothy Hammill haircut.
    b. The dust cloud that hangs over the top of an erupting volcano.
    c. An umbrella that won't turn inside out in the wind.
    d. Belly fat that flops over the top of low-rise jeans.

10. Swipeout (n.):
    a. A method of stealing merchandise.
    b. The gang term for a hit.
    c. An overdraft caused by using an ATM card recklessly.
    d. A credit card with the magnetic strip worn out.

(All answers are d. Give yourself 2,458,719 points for each correct answer. If you got 2,458,719 points, or more, you're one hip dude, and you're probably spending too much time in chatrooms or the employee lounge. If you didn't know any, then scratch your grundle, fix your wings, quit your newsfasting, and ask the nearest freshmore what percussive maintenance means.)

Questions and Answers

Q: *Dear Mrs. Adams,*

As you seem knowledgeable about the little things in life, I hope you might help me with my problem.

I love the beach. Our kids love the beach. My husband loves to pester me at the beach. Every summer he starts in about the same old thing: trying to get me into a bikini.

He tells me that I don't have many more years that I can still wear one in public. I guess he means that soon I will resemble an old hag, and he wants to view my scenery before he can't stand to look at it anymore.

His favorite line, "You would look better than her in a bikini," does not encourage me, since Jabba the Hut would look better than her in a bikini. Alan Alda would look better than her in a bikini. My husband would even look better than her in a bikini.

He also cleverly uses the tactic of pointing out to me women with whom I would compare favorably, in his mind's eye. Usually he picks out single twenty-somethings who haven't had anything, ever, fight its way out of their abdomens. My bellybutton no longer looks like a cute little "O." Its shape more reminds me of droopy oval holes in the stretched out earlobes of an old lady who wore twenty carat diamond earrings her whole adult life, only not so ritzy.

Should my children, as well as other unsuspecting tourists, suffer through my husband and, I'm certain, a myriad of other men ogling me in my teeny weenie yellow polka dot bikini?

Yours Truly,
B. Kheeny

A: *Dear B. Kheeny,*

You must consider two things in this situation. On the one hand you may sacrifice your children's innocence for the sake of your husband's satisfaction. On the other hand, once a person hits 35 she begins hurtling toward her final demise at an unfathomable rate and doesn't have much time remaining to let it all hang out, so to speak.

If you desire to put an end to your spouse's relentless barrage of bikini remarks, explain to him that children, boys in particular, do not want to ever in their entire lives think of their mother as "sexy," or think of anyone else thinking of her that way, not even their father. They want to believe their parents conceived them through a mortal form of immaculate conception and that they entered the world by osmosis. End of story.

Yet, at the same time, you might want to grasp hold of the final opportunity to expose a larger portion of your flesh to the sun than you have in years, while you still appeal to your spouse. Don't fear the bumps, bulges and sags. Tanning fat and flab converts it instantaneously to muscle. It's an established fact.

So you don't feel comfortable with a bikini now, in a few years you might decide to give it a try. Your time frame for exhibitionism extends far beyond your husband's imagination. I've seen fossils on the beach, and I know for a fact that they wear the dreaded two-piece. Their skin looks like leather and they pull up their knees to sit down in a beach chair. Children intently search the sand for their teeth.

All this said, a good rule of thumb is to wear a bathing suit that makes you and your daddy feel comfortable.

Fan Mail

I routinely review fan mail from dedicated readers and pass complaints on to a grievance committee, which evaluates each one for validity, recommends remediation, and sends readers a full report of the investigation. Expect results, but don't wait on tenterhooks, as sitting on them over an extended period of time can create oozing sores. If you wish, you may e-mail your own questions to lucybgoosey@aol.com.

Some readers, however, merely pose questions. These I can easily answer:

Dear "Miss" Lucy,

You mention cats quite often. Perhaps you can aid me with a feline problem of my own. You see, several cats have taken up residence under my steps, causing the entry of my abode to smell like a squatting ground, if you catch my odiferous drift.

I would like to move the brood to my barn, where, hopefully, they will develop into marvelous mousers. Unfortunately, the scratching, hissing, clawing critters won't come out, unless I open the front door, and only get feistier when I poke them with a stick.

Any ideas?
Sincerely,
Kitty Lettier

Dear Ms. Lettier,

Here, here Kitty, Kitty. The way I see it, if you can't get the litter out of the box, throw on more sand, if you catch my devious drift. I offer the following suggestions:
1. Shoot them; then pick them up and move them to the barn.
2. Crouch inside the front door holding a burlap bag. Casually swing the door wide enough for the cats to dart directly into the waiting sack. Cinch the sack, twist your mustache, and consider the endless possibilities.
3. Perhaps you have a problem with mice, not cats. Set traps in your barn. The cats would eventually return to their haven under your steps anyway, and you will still have to shoot them.

Dear "Miss" Lucy,
I think my mother lost her mind. I'm in third grade, and over the

course of my nine years she seems to have deteriorated rapidly. The other day she picked us up from school, brought us home and fed us cookies and milk. (Doesn't she know this is the 2000's. Kids eat Twinkies, drink cola and watch TV after school. Duh!)

Shortly thereafter, the phone rang.

My mom lifted the receiver and blurted, "Oh, this must be the school. I'm so sorry. I completely forgot to get the kids. I'll be there right away." Then she hung up, turned around and startled when she saw me.

Is my mom losing it?

Truly yours,
A. Cy Lumn

Dear Little Lumn,

She needs you and your siblings to clean your rooms every day, do the dishes every night, quit bickering forever, and give her privacy in the bathroom.

Try this, and I assure you that when your youngest sibling leaves for college, she will fully recover. In the meantime, Twinkies and Coke will rot your teeth.

Dear "Miss" Lucy,

My family has an on-going argument about acetone. None of us can agree on its meaning. My dad says it's ant killer. My sister says it's nail polish remover. My grandmother says it's fitness equipment.

Could you end this dispute once and for all? (P.S. I've got money riding on this.)

All the best,
Ace

Dear Ace,

You and your family members have missed the hole on this one. Acetone describes a physique. For example, when a hot chick walks by, you might shout, "Ooh girl, your acetone!" Or the auctioneer at a donkey sale might lead the bidding by saying, "We've got a strong specimen here, folks. This acetone."

By the by, your wife told me that, because you bet on this ridiculous disagreement, you're acegrass.

(And she's going to tuck your skirt in your panties, too.)

Postlogue

Dainty Leave-Taking

A few things I'm not:
1. I'm not graceful at accepting praise or gifts.
2. I'm not bored.
3. I'm not making up any of this.
4. I'm not my husband's mother.
5. I'm not ever going to re-heat a hardboiled egg in the microwave, again.
6. I'm not getting any younger.
7. I'm not alone.
8. I'm not making my happiness depend on someone else.
9. I'm not wasting my words.
10. I'm not good at good-byes.

One of the last books I read was by Garrison Keillor, *Lake Woebegon Summer* 1956. I bought it used in a bookstore in Costa Rica. On a warm, early spring day, I sat in a rocking chair on the front porch to finish it, only to discover that it had the saddest ending ever. I nearly cried.

Page 286 ended, "- and the next morning he came to his . . ." No page 237. Just blam! Over. Right in the middle of a sentence. I lay awake that night wondering, *came to his what - aid, mother's house, senses, funeral? What?* It's enough to drive me right back down to Costa Rica to find the missing page.

Now that would be a happy ending, a fine farewell - me off to the tropics with my skirt tucked in my panties.

One of the most important southern social graces is to know when to go. As my mama always put it, "You be careful not to wear out your welcome." Whether southern or not, all the great writers knew when to quit. They knew the exact placement of The End that would keep them from saying too much, yet keep the reader salivating for more. Wordsmiths such as these are acclimated to poetic departures:

Let us not be dainty of leave-taking.
  - Shakespeare

This was I,
a sparrow.
I did my best;
farewell.
  - William Carlos Williams

My friends — No one, not in my situation, can appreciate my feeling of sadness at this parting. To this place, and the kindness of these people, I owe every thing . . . I now leave, not knowing when, or whether ever, I may return . . . To His care commending you, as I hope in your prayers you will commend me, I bid you an affectionate farewell.
  - Abraham Lincoln

Good night, good night. Parting is such sweet sorrow . . .
  - William Shakespeare, *Romeo and Juliet*

And so to bed.
  - Samuel Pepys

Unfortunately, I often fail to heed the advice of my mother, as well as the example of writers who have gone on before me. The missing page bothers me far less than an ending completed. I have no affinity for finality.

I am the reason that party hosts print on the invitation the exact hour their event will end. My friends affectionately call me the hanger-on-er because I like to stay until the last pig in a blanket disappears from the platter. I can't help thinking that if I leave too soon, I might miss something more exciting than paying the babysitter and driving her home. Plus, I know hanging around keeps people from talking about me.

There are some obvious signs to look for, however, to know when the party is absolutely over:

1. Someone asks you to help clear the dishes from the buffet.
2. Your host is snoring in front of ESPN.
3. Your spouse is standing over you jingling his keys in his pocket.
4. The wine box runs dry.
5. Your husband reports that there's no more beer.
6. A stranger asks if you can hold her hair while she pukes.
7. You haven't been seen with your husband for so long that women begin treating him like he's single.
8. People start talking about politics, religion, or how best to educate children.
9. The stereo goes silent.
10. The hostess releases the hound from the guest bedroom.
11. Another party-goer, too inebriated to drive himself home, calls dibs on the sofa you're sitting on.
12. Someone turns out the kitchen light, the living room light, the den light, the front porch light . . .

I am not and have never been good at saying good-bye. The best farewell, in my mind, is one not said. I would rather slip away in the night with no formal conclusion. So-long: so final; it leaves no room for error, for perhaps rendezvousing again.

Farewell, farewell, you old rhinoceros,
I'll stare at something less prepoceros.
    - Ogden Nash

And so, alas, farewell. I will make my exit while you're not looking. Please forgive me my character flaw.

Adieu, adieu, adieu! Remember me.
    - Shakespeare, *Hamlet*

Lucy Adams

Lucy Adams is a graduate of the University of Georgia. She received her Master's degree from Augusta State University, then returned to the University of Georgia for doctoral studies. She left her doctoral program to become an over-educated housewife and mother of four children. Lucy later returned to work in the field of education.

Lucy writes a weekly humor column for newspapers in Georgia and Tennessee, as well as freelance magazine articles on family and parenting topics. She is also the author of the highly successful book, *If Mama Don't Laugh, It Ain't Funny*. She lives in Thomson, GA. Despite that, she is always cold, which she says is more a state of being than a personal stat. She copes. Learn more about Lucy and all of her projects at:

www.IfMama.com

Special thanks to the folks at Palm Tree Press for supporting me in my second book with them. Their confidence in *Tuck Your Skirt* has made all the difference.

Thank you to all of my friends and family, and the strangers, too, who find themselves featured in this book. I am hopeful that no lawsuits will be brought against me. It isn't slander if it's true, right?

Special thanks to Helen, Alan, the Paiges, Charlotte, and Greg who keep me supplied with plenty of material, some of it too weird to even include in this book. I would be remiss if I also didn't mention Jeannie and Anne Marie who have kept me laughing in the teachers' lounge over the years. I would mention my family members by name here, but they might get mad and hold it against me and quit putting me in the Christmas drawing.

Sincere gratitude to the town of Thomson, GA and all the citizens who count me as one of their own, even though, by their terms, I am a relative newcomer. I am proud to say I hail from this fair town.

And, finally, thanks to [your name here], who read right through to the acknowledgements. Your dedication and fortitude are greatly appreciated.

LaVergne, TN USA
17 January 2011

212644LV00004B/5/P